THE INEXPLICABLE LAWS OF SUCCESS

Discover the Hidden Truths that Separate the 'Best' from the 'Rest' (Classic Edition)

Published by
Ink 'n Ivory Pty Ltd
P O Box 6321, Rouse Hill, NSW. 2155. Australia
www.inkNivory.com
Blog: www.CoolSelfHelpTips.com

ISBN: 978-1-922113-03-0 (Paperback)
ISBN: 978-1-922113-04-7 (Hardcover)
ISBN: 978-1-922113-05-4 (ePub)
ISBN: 978-1-922113-06-1 (Mobi)

First Printing: 2013
First Revision: 2025

Disclaimer
This publication is shared with the understanding that the publisher and author are not engaged in rendering financial, psychological, or any other professional service and are offered for information purposes only. If financial or any other professional advice or assistance is required, the services of a competent professional person should be sought. The reader is solely responsible for his/her actions arising from using this document.

Dedication

To Caitlyn, James, Alaska, and Avalon:

This book – it's for you, with all the love we've gathered along the wild, unpredictable road called life.

Ralph Waldo Emerson once said, "What lies behind us and what lies before us are *tiny* matters compared to what lies <u>within</u> us." Tiny... but also huge, right? Everything inside you, all that potential, it's a universe waiting to burst open. This book? It's a nudge, a guide, a reminder that you're capable of more than you think.

Now, life's not a straight line – it's messy, full of twists and turns, but that's where the fun is. You'll face challenges (big ones, little ones, the sneaky ones), and when you do, come back to these pages. Let them remind you that you have the power to shape your own story, no matter what.

Purpose, happiness, success – those big, elusive words – they're yours to define.

We hope these ideas give you the strength to stumble, rise, and discover who you really are. And maybe, just maybe, they'll help you make your mark on this world in a way only you can.

With more love and admiration than words can say,

Verusha Robbins – Mom / Aunty Vushie

Virend Singh – [Grand]Pa

TWO QUICK TIPS TO MAXIMIZE YOUR LEARNING

TIP 1

As you discover the life-enhancing principles and strategies in *The Inexplicable Laws of Success*, you will likely feel inspired to apply these concepts and start seeing real results in your life. That's where the companion workbook comes in – a powerful tool with exercises, prompts, and space for reflection to help you take your learning to the next level. By working through the workbook, you'll be able to apply the laws of success in a more intentional and meaningful way, accelerating your progress and achieving the breakthroughs you've been seeking. Don't just read about success – experience it for yourself. Get your copy of the workbook today at the following link: https://Chosen4U.com/TilosWB/

TIP 2

As you embark on this journey to discover the secrets of success, I want to share a life hack I found years ago.

While reading this e-book, I highly recommend pairing it with the audiobook version. By listening to the audiobook alongside the e-book, you'll be able to:

- Absorb the material more efficiently
- Retain more information
- Apply the principles to your life more effectively
- Experience a more immersive and engaging learning experience

To get started, secure your copy of the audiobook version of *The Inexplicable Laws of Success* from the options provided at the following link: https://Chosen4U.com/TilosAudio/

Acknowledgements

Writing this book has been a journey – one that would not have been possible without the support, wisdom, and generosity of many incredible individuals. We are deeply grateful to all those who have played a role in bringing this project to life.

First, we extend our heartfelt appreciation to the spiritual teachers, past and present, whose insights have shaped our understanding of the world. Their wisdom has guided, challenged, and inspired much of what we share in these pages.

We also want to acknowledge the self-help authors, coaches, and thought leaders whose work has enriched our thinking. Their diverse perspectives have contributed to our growth, and we are grateful for the knowledge they have shared.

A special thank you goes to the authors, poets, and storytellers whose words appear in this book. While some sources remain elusive, we have done our best to credit the original creators. Their powerful messages add depth and meaning to our work, and we are truly thankful.

To those who took the time to review our manuscript and offer feedback – we appreciate you more than words can express. In particular, we are deeply grateful to Aroona Naidoo for her meticulous editing of our first draft. We also sincerely thank Carol Thomas, Christine Dominguez, Alicia Morrison, Jan and Steve Osmond, Greg Mickan, Kathy Hume, Ravi Naik, Daniel Levis, and Eshwar Vasista. Your encouragement, insights, and belief in this book have been invaluable.

Finally, to every reader who picks up this book – thank you. Your curiosity, openness, and desire for growth are what make this journey worthwhile.

With deep gratitude,

Verusha and Virend

About This Book

By John Harricharan
Award-winning author of the best-seller
When You Can Walk on Water, Take the Boat.

One of the most amazing books I've come upon lately is *The Inexplicable Laws of Success*, written by a father and daughter team, Virend Singh and Verusha Robbins. Now, you might think, with so many books being written about success and its variations, there is nothing about this topic that would really hold my attention for long.

But you'd be wrong.

After just a few pages, I found myself caught up in the subject matter. I discovered (or re-discovered) many eternal truths in the ensuing chapters. The authors have a way of taking complex ideas and distilling them into a simple roadmap. I was equally enthralled by the pertinent stories the authors used to illustrate various points.

The Inexplicable Laws of Success is a book with the potential to change countless lives. The wisdom and pragmatic advice in this volume could benefit everyone. In some ways, it is a magical book that combines ancient wisdom with practical, modern methods.

Read *The Inexplicable Laws of Success* often. Keep it on your desk so you can refer to it time and again. Don't leave it on your bookshelf to gather dust. Make it a part of your life.

Thank you, Virend and Verusha, for giving such a valuable and useful book to the world. I, for one, am grateful and hope you'll write many more volumes for us.

What readers say about this book:

"This book gives you ideas and insights into unlocking and releasing your full potential for happiness and success."

**~ Brian Tracy,
International Best-Selling Author**

"Powerful, unlike any other self-help book. It's sheer brilliance in the way it distills pertinent information and explains the Universal Laws of Success. It starts by explaining your divine connection with the Universe. It then describes the Law of Attraction in a refreshing new way using a trademarked concept called the Success Continuum®. This is followed by a clarification of the concept of 'BE, DO, and HAVE' and a detailed explanation of the Law of Being, the Law of Doing, and the Law of Having, all of which are brought to a magnificent close with yet another trademarked concept called the Ultimate Success Formula®. Prepare to be enlightened and inspired every step of the way."

**~ Aroona Naidoo,
Educator and Reiki Master**

"It is said that the best books are not written yet. They are still in the hearts and minds of people. The Inexplicable Laws of Success is perhaps such a book. It has transcended the hearts and minds of its authors and been transformed into print. It has immense value. Cherish it!"

**~ Christine Dominguez,
Media Coordinator for Hay House Australia**

"This is one of the most complete books on success that I have ever read. It combines elements of self-help, spirituality, business, and philosophy in a most remarkable way. Thoroughly enjoyable and inspiring. I highly recommend it to anyone ready to usher in lasting, positive change into their lives."

**~ Ravi Naik
(Engineer, 'Compassionate Samurai')**

"WOW!! – It is indeed fascinating, compelling reading. I have read it cover to cover. I believe it is a compendium of the collective wisdom of the ages. It is easy to read, written in simple English language, explanation of some complex concepts and phenomenon are convincing and influential. It is a manual that can be used as a step-by-step guide for self-development and improvement. I believe it should be made compulsory reading for all high school students."

~ Eshwar Vasista (Engineer, Entrepreneur)

"Fascinating, as it is powerful. The Inexplicable Laws of Success would benefit every coach (regardless of discipline), every entrepreneur, every speaker, every teacher, every parent... and everyone else not mentioned."

~ Alicia Morrison
(Owner: Morrison Consulting)

"New and different... very different! It shows the path to success from a completely unique perspective. Study it and reach your highest goals and aspirations with greater ease and confidence."

~ Samuel Tesfay
(Owner: Silva Method Australia Pty Ltd)

"When presented with The Inexplicable Laws of Success, I said to myself, "Oh, no; not another self-help book!" Then I read the book, and what an awakening it was. If you have dreams for greater success in life, make it a priority to read this book. You will make a quantum leap in your understanding of success!"

~ Peter Turnbull (Actor, Educator)

"The authors, Virend Singh and Verusha Robbins, are virtually unknown in the self-help realm, but certainly not unknowing when it comes to self-help concepts. They have done an exceptional job explaining the subtle things, or rather, the hidden truths that separate the 'best' from the 'rest.'"

~ Matthew Morey (Owner, Salmacis)

"This book is a game-changer. It contains timeless truths that all of us should embrace. Read it, and you will attain a whole new perspective about reality and what it takes to live more effectively."
~ Jim Gribilas (Business Coach, Entrepreneur)

"This book is for every person aspiring to live an enriched, meaningful, and fulfilling life. It educates; it enlightens; it motivates; it inspires; it entertains; and, most importantly, it awakens your spirit to live life more effectively. It's one of a kind. Enjoy!"
~ Rita Amarasinghe (Accountant)

"Profound! Knowing the authors as I do, I am not surprised at the insightful and practical nature of the information provided."
~ Bala Balakrishnan
(Owner, Director: Source2win Pty Ltd)

"This book contains all the ingredients for anyone, regardless of their current position in life, to be able to enjoy a lifestyle of abundance. It is comprehensive and well researched, but at the same time clear, concise, and easy to follow."
~ Greg Mickan (Roo Marketing)

"The Inexplicable Laws of Success takes you on a journey, the journey of 'success.' It will teach you exactly what it takes to be successful in life regardless of what success means to you. I wish I had learned the information contained in this book when I was still a teenager. My life would be a whole lot more enriching."
~ Kresant Mahilall
(Director at Rank Higher)

"I am continually amazed by Verusha's passion to assist individuals in their personal growth. She writes in a way that is motivating and inspirational."

~ Deepak Chopra,
International Best-Selling Author

Contents

The Adventure Begins

Imagine standing at the starting line of the most thrilling game ever created – life itself! Not just any game, but one where you get to write the rules as you learn them. Crazy, right? That's exactly what "The Inexplicable Laws of Success" is about. It's your personal playbook for mastering this wild ride, unlocking potential you might not even know you have.

You know how some games seem impossible until someone shows you the secret moves? Life's somewhat like that. While spiritual texts, motivational talks, and maybe something on social media give us glimpses of wisdom about finding joy and peace (and those are super important!), they don't quite hand us the complete manual for navigating life's crazy maze. Maybe there isn't one perfect guidebook – we're all writing our chapters as we go.

But here's something amazing – you're on a journey of self-discovery, with new levels of understanding and growth waiting for you at every turn. Whether you're just starting out or already well on your way, there's always another level, another achievement to unlock. That's what makes this whole journey so fascinating.

This is where "The Inexplicable Laws of Success" emerges as your trusty companion. You were intuitively guided here because something deep within compels you towards change and self-discovery. This is no mere coincidence; this book has arrived just when you need it most, holding the keys to transforming your life.

A Fresh Look at Success

What the heck is success anyway? It's not the same for everyone. For some, success might mean wealth and fame. For others, it might be the joy of a fulfilling relationship, the pride of academic achievement, or finishing that one project that's been haunting them.

But real success? It goes way beyond that. It's about achieving something that brings real meaning and fulfillment. Success isn't just outward achievements; it's living a life that resonates with your deepest values and purpose.

You've likely heard the saying, "There's nothing new under the sun." Don't let it fool you. True, the core principles of success might have been around for ages, but this book breaks through the noise with a radically new approach. We're not regurgitating what you've heard before. Nope. We're giving you something that will flip how you see your path to success, distilling it into something that finally clicks.

Each chapter is carefully crafted to reveal the hidden laws that influence your success, and how they connect to form a complete, actionable roadmap for your life. These ideas will help you see success in a way that's simple, clear, and, most importantly, achievable.

Completing Your Map

Everyone has a map they use to navigate life – a mental model of how the world works. But for most people, that map is incomplete. No wonder it's so easy to feel lost or frustrated. This book? It's the missing parts of your map, the pieces that are going to bring the whole picture into focus.

Through powerful stories, vivid examples, and timeless wisdom, we'll uncover the hidden truths about success that most people don't even notice. You'll learn not only from the greatest thinkers of the past and present, but also from our personal experiences. We don't limit ourselves to any one belief system or doctrine. Instead, we honor the wisdom found in all traditions, East and West, while maintaining a universal approach to success.

As you journey through these pages, be prepared to challenge your current thinking. Just because an idea is new doesn't mean it's untrue. In fact, the ideas we resist most often hold the greatest potential for growth.

Imagine never having seen the stars before. Now imagine someone pointing to the clear blue sky on a sunny day, telling you countless bright stars existed beyond Earth's atmosphere. You might think they are wacko, but once night falls, and you gaze up at the star-studded expanse above, you'll be awestruck and mesmerized. Your whole worldview changes in an instant!

The principles in this book are like those stars – at first, they may seem unfamiliar or even unbelievable, but once you experience them, you'll be amazed at how they can change your life.

So, as you embark on this journey, we encourage you to keep an open mind. Take your time, reflect, and be willing to embrace new ideas. The principles in this book have the potential to help you achieve what may have once seemed impossible.

What's so "Inexplicable" about Success?

People often scratch their heads trying to figure out why some folks seem to dance through life while others struggle. It's like there are these invisible forces at work – and honestly, sometimes there are! How else can one explain:

- How the universe seems to throw you a bone right when you refuse to give up?
- Or that weird thing where believing in something impossible somehow makes it possible?
- What about when you give without expecting anything back, and life dumps a truckload of good stuff in your lap?
- And don't even get us started on those "coincidences" that line up so perfectly they can't possibly be random!

We'll dig into all this stuff throughout the book. When we say "inexplicable," we don't mean these things can't be understood – just that they're sneaky. They work in ways that might not make sense at first glance. Through careful examination, we can demystify even the most perplexing aspects of extraordinary achievement.

The Truth Revealed: Success is Predictable!

The power to succeed lies in acknowledging that there are universal laws or principles governing achievement. These principles are not reserved for a select few – they work for everyone, everywhere, every time. Just like gravity doesn't play favorites, these principles don't care about your background or circumstance. This means that true success is within your grasp, waiting to be unlocked.

Legendary self-development author Brian Tracy once said, "Success is as predictable as the sun rising in the east and setting in the west." This isn't an exaggeration; it's an inspiring truth! Achieving success is much like baking: if you follow the recipe correctly, you'll get a cake – every time.

Success is a predictable outcome based on your actions and choices. Some behaviors propel you toward your desired outcomes, and others hinder your progress. Study successful people – really *study* them – and you'll find they don't just get lucky. They follow patterns, habits, and ways of thinking that anyone can replicate.

Small Changes, Big Rewards

The power of incremental improvements is evident all around us – often, it's the tiniest tweaks, the smallest changes, that make the biggest difference. Consider a horse race where the winner, finishing just a nose ahead (finishing just the length of its nose in front of the horse that comes next), earns millions more than the second-place finisher. That's exactly what happened in the 2011 Melbourne Cup. Dunaden won by the narrowest margin and pocketed $3.6 million, while the second-place finisher walked away with $900,000. A fraction of a second made that difference.

Life works the same way. That tiny edge – whether it's pushing yourself just a little harder or making one extra call – can end up flipping everything in your favor. The principles in this book? They're designed to help you make those subtle but powerful shifts that'll lead to something much bigger.

Virend's Journey

Let me share something personal here. For what feels like forever, I dreamed about living life on my own terms – you know, that magical mix of passion, freedom, and enough money to not worry about bills. So, I did what everyone says you're supposed to do: got the education, landed the good job(s), worked my tail off. And guess what? It wasn't enough.

Twenty-five years into my career, making what most would call "good money," I was stuck in this crazy cycle. Mortgage payments, car loans, credit card debt – it was like running on this endless treadmill of paying stuff off. Looking ahead, I could see retirement coming up fast, and unless something changed dramatically, I'd be stuck in this loop until the day I stopped working.

Talk about a wake-up call! It hit me like a freight train – I needed to make some serious changes.

You know that saying "be careful what you wish for"? Man, it's true. Through this weird chain of events (funny how life works), I stumbled onto this business opportunity. First reaction? Not interested… at all. But something made me take a second look and analyze it properly. Thank goodness I did, because that decision kicked off the craziest journey of personal growth I've ever experienced.

Those first two years? Pure chaos. Zero visible progress. Like trying to find your way through a maze in the dark. But in all that mess, two massive truths jumped out at me:

1. Want your life to get better? *You* have to get better.
2. Want prosperity? Create something of value for *other* people.

That's when the magic happens!

Yeah, I've had my share of failures and setbacks. But by learning from each mess-up and keeping at it, I built something amazing – a business that keeps generating income whether I'm working or not. Pure magic!

As I reflect on my journey, I'm reminded of Christopher Morley's wise words: "There is only one success – to be able to spend your life in your own way." For me, that meant business. For you? It could be something totally different. But here's the thing – whatever field you're targeting, you've got to study it inside and out. Want to be a great carpenter? Study carpentry. Want to be successful in life? Study success itself.

This book? It's my 25-year deep dive into what makes success tick. And sometimes, I still run into stuff I find difficult to explain – experiences that remind me there's something bigger than us pulling strings behind the scenes, helping our deepest dreams become real.

Verusha's Journey

Starting at the early age of eight, every Friday evening (except during school breaks), my dad ran a mentoring session for family and friends. He taught us about the incredible power of the mind and its boundless potential to achieve the miraculous. Those hours were filled with stories of extraordinary human achievements intertwined with the wisdom of philosophers and spiritual teachers, igniting our imaginations. Beyond mere storytelling, we were active participants, engaging in exercises to sharpen our focus and clarify our goals.

These formative years instilled in me a profound understanding of the transformative power of the mind and the art of visualizing success. I learned that our thoughts and words shape our reality, empowering me to achieve personal goals and contribute positively to the world around me.

Dad even turned my name into an acronym, giving it more meaning than it originally had:

> V = Visualize
> E = Emotionalize
> R = Realize
> U = U (you)
> S = Shall

H = Have
A = All

Cheesy? Maybe. But it worked! Now, every time I write it, I am reminded of those early lessons and what it takes to succeed in life.

Those Friday nights shaped my life in ways I can't fully explain. Looking back, I realize I subconsciously absorbed self-development and motivational wisdom, sometimes without even trying. Now, it's embedded in my DNA!

Dad's car was a mobile classroom, too. Without fail, there was always an audio tape or CD playing, with a motivational speaker sharing insights on life and success. It used to drive me up the wall!

As a teenager, all I wanted to do in the car was listen to music and tune out, which was impossible with that "annoying" Dr. Norman Vincent Peale, Og Mandino, or some other well-known expert blasting through the speakers. But, without realizing it, I started to internalize their wisdom until I could quote key phrases word for word. I soon began to believe the messages I heard, and they became 'friends'– an integral part of my identity!

As I grew older, I drew on what I had learned, and my life began to shift. I had aspirations to work for a reputable publishing company, and when I decided to join Hay House (Australia), a series of "coincidences" led me there.

Working for Hay House, I met, interviewed, and was privileged to write about authors who had inspired me during my formative years. It's moments like these that reinforce my belief in what I was taught, especially about the power of positive thinking to manifest a desired outcome.

I believe we all have a higher calling, a purpose that is intrinsically ours to follow if we so choose. This is part of mine – the gift of writing this book with my dad and sharing the precious lessons I've learned with you.

I hope this book takes you on an incredible journey, an adventure where you might scale your personal mountains, fight your fears, laugh unexpectedly, and discover the tremendous potential that lies within you.

A New Beginning

So here we are – at your starting line. Are you ready to discover just how powerful you really are and to uncover the laws that can help you create the life you've been dreaming about?

Remember, real success isn't about copying someone else's path – it's about spending your life in a way that feels true to you. This book is your guide to figuring out what that means and making it happen.

It's time to turn the page and begin your adventure.

PART 1

The Laws are Sacred

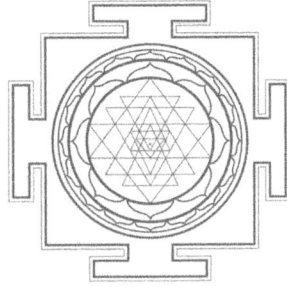

Chapter 1

Your Invisible Partner in Success

Picture having an extraordinary ally – one so powerful, so creative – it could shape your dreams into reality beyond anything you've envisioned. Sounds like a fantasy, right? But it's not. Stick with me here because this game-changer has slipped past many, yet it's accessible to anyone bold enough to reach out to it.

You already have this partner. In fact, it's been with you all along. The most wonderful collaborator you could ever imagine is standing by, ready to help you achieve your highest aspirations. The real tragedy? Most people go their entire lives unaware of this life-changing relationship.

This partner is vibrant, dynamic, and infinitely creative. It's on your side, rooting for you, yearning for your success even more than you do. And here's the kicker: it doesn't just cheer from the sidelines – it has the power to *orchestrate* your success. It can coordinate opportunities, resources, and people in ways you never thought possible. All it asks is that you acknowledge its presence, communicate your desires with heartfelt emotion, and commit to your goals with unyielding resolve.

This moment – right now – could be the turning point that changes everything. Recognizing and partnering with this invisible force might become the most defining decision of your life.

But let's make one thing clear: this isn't a servant or subordinate. Your invisible partner is *the Universe* itself. It's not here to work *for* you; it's here to work *with* you. Success isn't handed to you on a silver platter. You're a co-creator in this process. That means showing up, taking inspired action, and collaborating with the Universe rather than passively waiting for it to deliver results.

Prepare yourself – you're standing on the edge of a life-changing revelation. Step into this partnership with intention and trust, and watch as the extraordinary becomes your new reality. The Universe is ready. The question is: Are you?

The Wondrous Universe

To comprehend how the Universe can assist you in achieving your goals, we must first examine its nature and how it operates. Your success is inextricably linked to your understanding of the Universe and its mechanisms.

When you look closer at the Universe and the evolution of life, you realize there's obviously a higher intelligence directing creation. Creation is not accidental. There is absolute precision and order in the way the Universe operates. Look at nature and see the perfect, harmonious way it functions to keep a balance between all living things.

What we are experiencing is a cosmic power called *Universal Intelligence* or *Universal Consciousness*. It is this cosmic force that makes our hearts beat, changes the seasons, grows all life, and spins the Earth and the planets around the sun to give us day and night.

Now, consider our Earth. Earth is just one planet in our solar system within the vast Milky Way Galaxy. Our sun is one of the Milky Way's 200 billion stars. Then picture this: there are approximately 100-400 billion galaxies in the observable universe beyond our own.

The following three images will give you some perspective. Take a moment to understand the Earth's size compared to other planets in our awesome universe. Try to get a deeper perspective on just how small our Earth is on this scale.

Figure 1.1 shows the Earth in relation to the Sun, which is about 100 times wider than Earth.

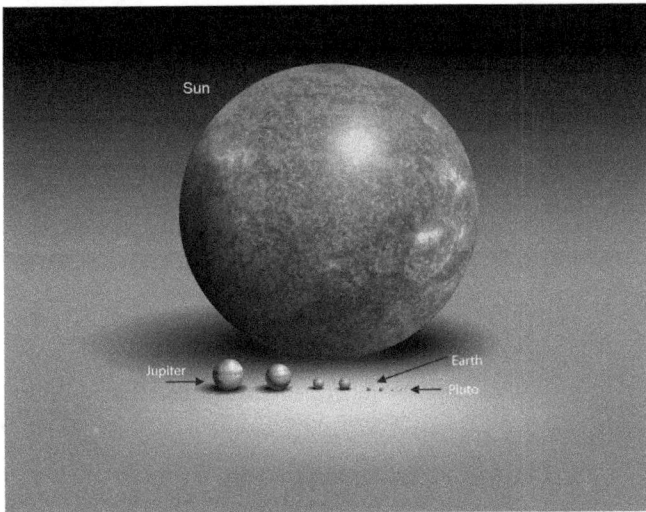

Figure 1.1

Figure 1.2 shows the Sun in relation to Arcturus, which is about 25 times wider than the Sun. Our Earth is invisible at this scale.

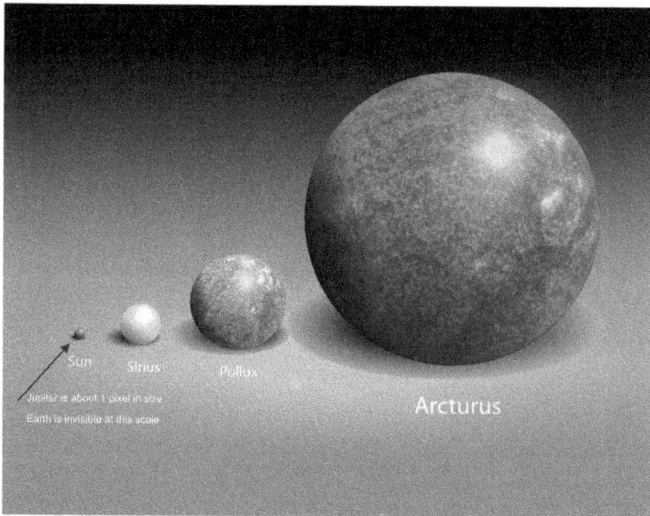

Figure 1.2

Figure 1.3 shows Arcturus in relation to Betelgeuse. The Sun is one pixel at this scale.

Figure 1.3

How much do you really know about this magnificent universe you live in?

Here are some facts that will blow your mind.

Betelgeuse (Figure 1.3) is a red supergiant star in the Milky Way (only part of which is shown in the picture above). It is about 1000 times wider than our Sun.

But Betelgeuse is not the largest known star!

One of the largest stars known (in terms of volume), and the largest in the Milky Way, is VY Canis Majoris (not shown). *Canis Majoris* means 'big dog' in Latin. It is about 500,000 times brighter and several billion times bigger than the Sun. According to Wikipedia, it would take 7 billion Suns to fill VY Canis Majoris.

The Sun, on the other hand, is about one million times bigger than Earth (in terms of volume). This means that you can fit a million Earths inside the Sun. Our Sun is just a tiny dot among several billion stars forming our Milky Way Galaxy. Our Earth feels like all there is to us, but we know it's just a tiny planet in a vast solar system in the Milky Way Galaxy.

In essence:

- Earth is one of many planets in our solar system, which comprises our Sun and everything that orbits around it, including planets, moons, asteroids, and other celestial objects.
- Our solar system is just one fragment of the vast Milky Way Galaxy.
- On average, each galaxy has 200 to 400 billion stars. (Our Sun is one of these stars.)
- The Milky Way is just one of more than 100 billion galaxies. Some estimates suggest there may be as many as 1-2 trillion galaxies in the observable Universe!

These comparisons illustrate the sheer magnitude of the cosmos. We inhabit a minuscule portion of an awe-inspiring Universe. In the grand scheme of things, Earth itself is a microscopic dot – barely noticeable!

You and the Universe

Despite the vastness of the cosmos, we are here for a specific reason. When we understand the reason, our doubts fall away, and it becomes our duty to live life *on* purpose and *with* a purpose.

The Universe's perfect order gives rise to the laws of nature that govern its operation. It is not likely that our orderly universe happened by chance. The earth is 150 million kilometers from the Sun. If Earth were much closer, it would burn up, and the oceans would boil away; if it were much farther away, Earth would freeze. Surely such a perfect organization requires a creative force. It is, therefore, very reasonable to believe that a supreme, intelligent force brought into existence the Universe, including the Earth and the wondrous diversity of life inhabiting it.

Regardless of what we call it or how science and religion define it, it's clear that there's a force out there, an intelligence or presence that operates mysteriously beyond its own creation.

Recognizing that this force exists is fundamental to our well-being.

People refer to this intelligent force by a wide variety of names, such as God, Allah, Christ, Krishna, Nature, Spirit, Creator, the Source, the Divine, Shunyata, Yahweh, Ein Sof, Gaia, Universal Consciousness, or simply as the Universe. We honor and respect all religious traditions equally, recognizing their sacred nature, while not promoting or favoring any particular faith. We use the terms God, the Universe, and *Universal Consciousness* interchangeably, depending on which is most appropriate at the time.

For a start, let's say that everything in existence, including you, is *Universal Consciousness* expressing itself in some form.

Let's take a closer look at this powerful concept.

You are Everything (A Revolutionary Perspective!)

All matter – everything in existence – is made up of atoms. We learned in school that the smallest unit of matter is an atom, which is like a tiny solar system. Imagine that! Is it a coincidence that the most microscopic atom and the macroscopic solar system have the same structural design?

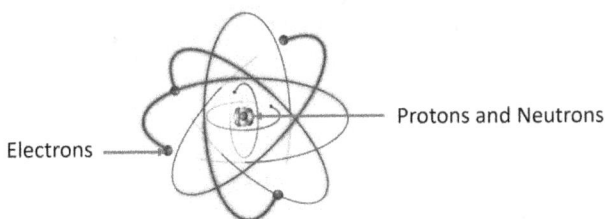

Electrons ——→

—— Protons and Neutrons

At the atom's core is the nucleus, consisting of a cluster of protons and neutrons, which make up 99.9% of the atom's mass. Smaller, lighter particles called electrons whirl at fantastic speeds around this nucleus.

To get an idea of the nature of an atom, imagine a football field. If the atom were magnified to the size of a football field, the nucleus would be smaller than the tip of a pen! The electron, which zips around the nucleus, would be smaller than a fleck of dust. But what the electron lacks in size, it makes up for in speed. According to Wikipedia, these electrons whiz around the nucleus at a rate of about 297,600 kilometers per second – the speed of light!

The electron moves so quickly around the nucleus that it gives the illusion of a solid shell. If you have ever moved a torch in a circular manner in the dark, it gives the illusion of a circle. This is precisely what the speedy electron does as it zips around the nucleus.

Since the nucleus constitutes 99.9% of the atom's mass (the "solid stuff"), the rest of the atom is essentially... nothing. It only appears larger due to the whizzing electron. Even more fascinatingly, the protons and neutrons within the nucleus aren't stationary – they, too, move about almost at the speed of light.

But here's where it gets truly mind-bending: the "solid" components of an atom – electrons, protons, and neutrons – aren't solid entities themselves. They're composed of subatomic particles with fancy names like quarks, leptons, and bosons. Scientists have discovered that these subatomic particles have particle-like and wave-like properties – yes, energy waves. So, in a way, nothing is truly solid anywhere!

Consider this: there's more empty space on a printed book page than actual "paper." The electrons in the atoms comprising the paper move so rapidly that they create the illusion of solid ink on solid paper. That perceived solidity is just that – an illusion. If all the electrons suddenly stopped moving, the sheet wouldn't merely crumble to dust; it would *disappear* into nothingness!

The Energy of "Oneness" That Connects Us All

Nothing is as solid as it appears; *everything is energy*. All matter is ultimately composed of energy. Everything in existence is made of the same stuff, just arranged differently. Everything in the universe affects everything else, binding us all in a profound *oneness* that goes beyond physical separation. We're all part of one big energy network... like a giant web. This is the single great Law of the Universe!

Here is a scientific fact: Everything constantly vibrates and pulsates, even seemingly immovable rock! The book (or e-book) you're reading vibrates energy, giving the illusion of solidity. We can't perceive these vibrations because our senses aren't attuned to frequencies of that speed. Everything you've ever seen, touched, heard, tasted, or smelled is simply the energy of different frequencies. This is also true of your body.

Here's something to wrap your head around:

Your body? It's basically a walking, talking, self-regulating symphony of systems – the skeletal, nervous, cardiovascular, respiratory, and a whole lineup of others working behind the scenes. But zoom in a little, and you'll find that at the core of all these systems are organs. Dig even deeper, and those organs? They're built from countless microscopic cells, the fundamental units of life itself.

Now, let's break it down further – cells are made up of molecules, tiny clusters of atoms bonded together. And what are atoms? The smallest units of matter, they are the invisible building blocks of *everything* in and around you. Take water, for example. One simple molecule of H_2O is just two hydrogen atoms (H) fused with one oxygen atom (O).

Here's where it gets particularly thought-provoking: Water makes up over 70% of your body. Meaning? The majority of *you* consists of hydrogen and oxygen atoms. But let's not stop there. Atoms themselves aren't solid microscopic balls; they're swirling pockets of energy, vibrating fields of subatomic particles behaving more like waves than fixed points in a given space.

So what does that make you? Not just flesh and bones, but a pulsating mass of energy, an intricate dance of charged particles, a living, breathing manifestation of pure consciousness. Fascinating, isn't it? Welcome to reality – where nothing is quite as solid as it seems.

Let us use an analogy to understand our connectedness with the Universe (or Universal Consciousness). Imagine for a moment that each of us is a tiny droplet of water, and Universal Consciousness is the entire ocean. This means that we are an intricate part of the whole, and the whole is part of each of us – there's no separateness, no duality. Like water droplets collectively forming the ocean, each of us is pure energy resonating and vibrating at our unique frequency – distinct from anything else in existence. This implies that everything, *including our thoughts and feelings*, vibrates at a certain frequency.

What Does Science Say?

Many in the scientific community agree that a creative power must exist behind the universe. Whether we perceive that power as God or simply the force of creation seems less crucial than acknowledging its existence.

Scientists have confirmed that we're all interconnected via energy. Research has shown that, at a subatomic level, each of us is influenced by literally everything around us, and we, in turn, influence everything else.

An intriguing experiment conducted by Soviet scientists in the 1960s dramatically illustrates our interconnectedness with everything in existence. While we don't endorse the experiment's methods, its results are profoundly revealing:

> A mother rabbit's newborn litter was placed aboard a submarine, which was then taken out to sea and submerged. The mother remained onshore; her brain activity (EEG readings) was carefully monitored. Beneath the water's surface, inside the submarine, the young rabbits were killed one by one. As each one perished, the mother's readings registered a reaction at the precise moment of each death. The experiment verified a tangible (or real) psychic link between living beings.
>
> (Pseudoscience Intelligence Studies, 2012)

Another fascinating experiment demonstrating our universal connectedness was conducted in 1993 under the direction of the United States Army Intelligence and Security Command (INSCOM):

> White blood cells (leukocytes) were scraped from the mouth of a volunteer, centrifuged, and placed in a test tube. A probe from a recording polygraph (a 'lie' or emotion detector) was inserted in the tube. The donor of the cheek cells was seated in a room separate from his donated cells and shown a television program with many violent scenes. When the volunteer viewed scenes of fighting and killing, the polygraph probe detected extreme excitation in the mouth cells of the donor, despite the test tubes being in a separate room down the hallway.

Subsequent repeats of the experiment with the donor and cells separated by up to fifty miles and up to two days after they were donated showed the same results. The donated cells remained energetically, and what scientists call 'non-locally,' connected with their donor and seemed to 'remember' where they came from.

(Pearsall, 1999)

Now that we've grasped the universe's colossal power and connectedness, how can we collaborate with it to attain success?

Working with the Universe

The answer lies in your intent and determination. When you crystallize your desires into a clear, unflinching focus and combine it with determined effort, you send a powerful signal to the Universe or Universal Consciousness. It's like tuning a radio to your desired frequency; the clearer the signal, the stronger the reception.

However, intent and determination alone are not enough. Your *emotions* are the fuel that ignites your desires. Yes, the Universe responds to human emotion – feelings of pain, pleasure, attraction, repulsion, enjoyment, distress, anger, fear, anticipation, and so on. Emotion is the *language* it understands. When you arouse emotions aligned with your desired outcomes, you raise your energy, making you a magnet for what you want.

Here's the crucial point: *You communicate with Universal Consciousness through your emotions!*

If you can fully grasp the meaning of this statement, then this may be your moment of truth – your 'aha' moment. Understanding this profound truth and harnessing the power of emotions to communicate your desires to Universal Consciousness can help you create outcomes beyond your wildest expectations – no exaggeration!

Universal Consciousness is dedicated to your personal advancement. This great power constantly seeks to express itself in some form; it strives to express itself *through you*. You are the medium for expression. Remember: This power works *through* and *with* you, but not *for* you. You are a *co-creator*; you work in partnership with Universal Consciousness.

The Power Is Within You

As you move forward, remember that success is not just a possibility – it's your birthright, waiting to be claimed through your partnership with the Universe. Your role is to provide the vision and passion; the Universe will supply the resources and opportunities.

Feel at ease knowing that the Universe is rooting for you. Every challenge is an opportunity for growth, and every setback is a preparation for a comeback. You are on an amazing journey, with the greatest adventure unfolding within you.

As you integrate these profound truths into your life, you'll begin to experience a shift in consciousness. Limitations will dissolve, and possibilities will expand. You'll discover a wellspring of inner strength and resilience that you never knew existed.

It's time to make some magic happen. The Universe awaits your command.

Hidden truths:

1. You already have a partner in success – the living Universe!
2. Acknowledging this partnership is vital for unlocking your potential.
3. Emotions are the key to communicating your desires to the Universe.
4. The Universe supports your chosen path.
5. You are limited only by the bounds of your imagination.

Chapter 2
The Unbreakable Laws of the Universe

Living a truly harmonious life means looking beyond the boundaries of human-made laws and connecting with something much greater. While the laws we follow in our countries provide order, there are deeper, Universal principles that guide all of existence. These principles shape everything, from the smallest speck of dust to the biggest stars.

Just as every nation operates under its own legal system, the Universe, too, operates under its own set of rules or laws. We refer to these as Universal Laws or Laws of Nature, *'whose content is set by nature and is therefore universal'* (Wikipedia).

These laws don't require your belief for them to work. They exist and operate whether you're aware of them or not, shaping how life flows with *absolute precision*. And when you go against them? You'll feel the consequences – there's no escaping their impact.

To live a happy and fulfilling life, you need to understand and comply with these Universal Laws. These laws are sacred. They are the foundation of everything in reality. These laws don't bend to *your* convenience or preference – they demand that you adapt, grow, and respect the order *they* provide. When you do, you'll find yourself in sync with the natural flow of life, opening the door to true harmony and fulfillment.

What Are the Universal Laws?

The Law of Gravity, a force with which we are all familiar, is a prime example of a Universal Law. So is the Law of Conservation of Energy, which states that energy cannot be created or destroyed, only transformed from one form to another. Unlike human laws, which can vary from country to country, Universal Laws are consistent and unchanging. You interact with these laws with every breath you take. They govern your existence. Nothing about your life has been casual or accidental!

The Universal Laws may seem mysterious, harboring hidden truths. When you identify and use these truths correctly, miracles or amazing results occur in your life. It may manifest as suddenly having money when you need it most, overcoming a life-threatening disease, or succeeding in a particular endeavor. These 'miracles,' no matter how incredible they might be, are not unbelievable outcomes. They are natural results of correctly applying specific laws of nature.

Unfortunately, some of the Universal Laws are not as clear-cut as they might seem. There are unnoticed subtleties to the Universal Laws, which, when understood and applied, can make all the difference between happiness and misery, prosperity and poverty, peace and conflict, ease and struggle.

It's easy to think that some people are born into affluence and that all good things happen to them. The truth is, these people aren't simply lucky; good things don't just *'happen'* to them. They're just applying the Laws of the Universe more effectively, whether they're aware of it or not. The laws are flawless, and they work perfectly every time. If you find that despite doing all the right things, your results are still poor, it's worth considering the Laws of the Universe and how you are applying them.

How many laws are there? Many. These laws govern every aspect of our existence. The supreme law of the Universe is the Law of Cause and Effect, also referred to as karma or the concept of *'reaping what you sow.'* This law states that for every effect, there is a cause, and for every action, there is a reaction. Positive actions lead to positive results. The Law of Cause and Effect operates regardless of time, space, or form, whether or not you are aware of it.

Every human thought, word, or deed is a *cause* that sets off a wave of energy throughout the Universe, resulting in either desirable or undesirable *effects*. If there are undesirable effects, it simply means that at some time in the past, there was a thought, word, or deed that caused a wave of undesirable energy. As normal, fully functioning people, we are quite literally responsible for everything in our lives. This concept is illustrated in the following excerpt.

> This is the suggestion a man gave to his subconscious mind over a period of about two years: *"I would give my right arm to see my daughter cured."* It appeared that his daughter had a crippling form of arthritis together with a so-called incurable form of skin disease. Medical treatment had failed to alleviate the condition, and the father had an intense longing for his daughter's healing and expressed his desire in the words just quoted.
>
> One day, the family was out for a drive. Their car was involved in a head-on collision. The father's right arm was torn off at the shoulder. When he came home from the hospital, he discovered that his daughter's arthritis and skin condition had vanished.
>
> (Murphy, 2001)

This story might seem extreme, but it powerfully demonstrates the Law of Cause and Effect in action – the father's intense desire, expressed through his words, manifested in a literal and unexpected way.

The Principle of Karma

Everyone is subject to the same natural Laws of the Universe, regardless of race, color, creed, or gender. They exert their influence without our consent or awareness. When we choose our behavior, we're also choosing the consequences. People who are frustrated in life consistently try to defy natural laws. Conversely, successful people live in harmony with the natural Laws of the Universe.

Deepak Chopra, a renowned authority in mind-body medicine, put it beautifully in his book "The Seven Spiritual Laws of Success":

> *No debt in the universe ever goes unpaid. There is a perfect accounting system in this universe, and everything is a constant "to and fro" exchange of energy.*

All of life is interconnected; what we do to others, we do to ourselves. According to the principle of karma, any negative or positive thought or action remains that way until it expends (uses up) its energy by acting upon the originator. The energy you create through your thoughts, words, and deeds – either negative or positive – will rebound and act on *you*. But, as it is the nature of energy to expand when it is put out into the world, you will, at some point, experience much more than you caused others to experience.

If you contribute to the prosperity and well-being of others, you will receive the same positive energy in return, often multiplied. Similarly, if you harm someone, that negative energy will eventually come back to cause you even greater harm, unless you make amends in some way.

Eighteenth-century German poet and philosopher, Wolfgang Von Goethe wrote:

> *Nature understands no jesting; she is always true, always serious, always severe; she is always right, and the errors and faults are always those of man. The man incapable of appreciating her, she despises and only to the apt, the pure, and the true, does she resign herself and reveal her secrets.*

The Unbreakable Laws of the Universe

The Law of Cause and Effect is the *iron law* of the Universe. It is unyielding. If you defy this law, there will be consequences – no *'ifs, ands, or buts'* about it. It's fascinating (and often tragic) to observe how many of us try to defy this law, especially when we pursue quick and easy gains. Often, we strive for what we want by doing the exact opposite of what is in our best interest.

This enchanting fable illustrates the mystifying and sometimes elusive workings of the Law of Cause and Effect.

A young man ventured into the forest and approached his spiritual master, with a heartfelt plea: "I yearn for boundless wealth, not for my own sake, but to serve and benefit the world. "What is the secret to wealth?" he inquired.

The wise master replied, "Within every human heart reside two Goddesses: The Goddess of Wealth and the Goddess of Knowledge."

Although you may hold affection for both, you must devote yourself to one while forsaking the other. Choose one Goddess to pursue. Shower her with love and give her your undivided attention. Having said that, understand that only the Goddess of Wealth can bestow riches upon you. Choose carefully, for you cannot pursue both.

But, here lies the secret: If you pursue the Goddess of Wealth, she will be pleased with your pursuit, for she delights in being chased. The more you pursue her, the more elusive she becomes. However, should you pursue the Goddess of Knowledge, the Goddess of Wealth will grow intensely jealous and turn her attention towards you. As you seek knowledge, the Goddess of Wealth will seek you. She will never abandon you, showering you with material blessings to win your favor, and the wealth you desire will be yours eternally.

Adapted from (Chopra, 1993)

The story conveys the counterintuitive idea that focusing on acquiring knowledge, not wealth directly, might lead to unexpected abundance.

The human tendency is to pursue 'Wealth', which seems like the logical choice. However, wealth is simply an *effect*, and like any effect, it has a *cause*. In the fable, pursuing one goddess gets you the best of both worlds; wealth comes from the acquisition and proper application of knowledge.

Let's clarify: Your goals and dreams will materialize when you are in harmony with the Laws of the Universe. It is a scientific fact that the Universe operates in absolute harmony with irrevocable natural laws and principles that have never varied throughout all time. These laws prevail regardless of whether we heed them or not. Those who live in accordance with the Laws of the Universe will ultimately succeed. Bestselling author Bob Proctor summed it up perfectly when he said,

> *You are living and working in a dynamic global marketplace that leaves little room for error. In the future, only those individuals whose beliefs are sound, in harmony with the laws of the universe, and have been integrated with their behavior, will emerge as real winners. (Proctor, 2011)*

You Have Unlimited Creative Ability

This much we know with certainty: you have unlimited potential, and you can tap into and harness this potential by combining:

1. A deeper understanding of yourself (your power of attraction) with
2. Specific efforts toward a desired outcome (your power of action).

In other words, you'll experience the rewards (the Law of *Receiving*) when you truly understand that you have immense, untapped ability, and you combine that understanding with deliberate application of the Law of *Attraction* and the Law of *Action*.

As we wrap up this chapter, I invite you to pause and contemplate the extraordinary reach and implications of the Universal Laws. These laws aren't arbitrary rules devised by humans but the blueprint of existence itself. By grasping and aligning with these laws, you'll unlock the power to shape your life in ways you may have never before imagined.

As you move forward, remember that you're not at the mercy of external circumstances but a co-creator with the Universe itself. Every thought, word, and action you choose sends ripples through the universe, shaping your future experiences. This knowledge is both empowering and sobering. It puts the responsibility for your life squarely in your hands while also providing you with the tools to create the life you've always dreamed of.

The following chapters explore practical strategies for leveraging the Laws of Attraction, Action, and Receiving. Pay particular attention to these laws, for they hold the keys to unlocking your limitless potential and the abundance that's your birthright.

Your journey toward unparalleled success and fulfillment begins now.

Hidden Truths:

1. The Law of Cause and Effect spans all space, time, and form. It operates whether you are aware of it or not.
2. Every thought, word, or deed is a *cause* that sets off a wave of energy, resulting in desirable or undesirable *effects*.
3. The energy you create through your thoughts, words, and deeds, whether negative or positive, will come back multiplied and act on *you*!

PART 2

The Law of Attraction

Chapter 3

You Are a Living Magnet - Align Your Power to Work for You

You are unique! There is no one else like you. Your existence is a remarkable expression of life and energy that has never been seen before and will never be replicated again. You may think that it's arrogant to think of yourself as important, but you are!

Why are you important?

Because you, in your unique way, are a necessary part of the universe's evolution with a purpose that only you can fulfill. You are meant to be here, in this moment, with all your strengths and weaknesses, with all your passions and fears. If you weren't, you wouldn't be here.

It's a waste of time to complain or compare yourself to others. Instead, see life as an opportunity to learn and grow, and contribute to the evolution of the universe that has been going on for the past 13.7 billion years.

Still, your path is your own. You have been dealt a unique and carefully selected set of cards, so play your hand as well as you can. Much like poker, it's not always the person with the best hand who wins; it's the person who plays their hand the best!

In the game of life, the same rule applies.

Perhaps life didn't hand you the role you wanted. Maybe you would have rather been someone like Oprah Winfrey, Steve Jobs, or the Dalai Lama. Who knows, that could still be in the cards for you! Just because their paths differ from yours doesn't mean they're better. They have their own challenges, and often they're pretty big ones. It's through facing and surmounting these challenges that they've gotten to where they are.

Each setback you face has the potential to bring about an equal or even greater advantage. Your job is to grow and learn from every situation. Who knows what the future holds for you? For now, the life you're living right now is not one to squander. You have the ability to be, do, and achieve anything you desire. To tap into this innate power, you must first recognize that it exists.

You Are Divine

A Hindu legend beautifully illustrates the divine power that exists within each of us.

There was a time when humans wielded divine powers, but due to misuse, Lord Brahma, the creator god, decided to hide them in a place where they would be impossible to find.

A council of lesser gods pondered suitable hiding places. One suggested burying them deep within the earth, but Lord Brahma countered that humans would eventually unearth them.

Another proposed sending their divinity to the ocean's depths, but again, he warned that exploration would eventually lead to their rediscovery.

After much thought, the lesser gods became concerned and declared, "Since human's divine powers cannot be safely concealed in either land or sea, then there is nowhere to hide them!"

Lord Brahma, with a knowing smile, proclaimed, "We shall hide them within humankind itself! For there, one never thinks to look."

Since then, the legend claims, humans have searched tirelessly for something that has always resided within them: their own divinity. This tale serves as a powerful reminder that our true potential, our divine spark, lies dormant within, waiting to be discovered and awakened.

(Baba, 2005)

It is also written that people are created in the same image and likeness of God. You might be familiar with the following quote:

Ye are Gods, and the spirit of God dwells within you.
~ Corinthians 3:16

This means that you are divine. You were born this way and will always remain so. Your soul is the individualized essence of the Divine. Often, our divinity is hidden beneath layers of fear, doubt, uncertainty, sorrow, rage, unworthiness, and false assumptions from past experiences. It's our responsibility to strip away these limiting beliefs and realize that our true power lies within, hidden not in the external world, but in the depths of our own being.

The power you hold within you is astounding. We have never been as close to understanding our true nature and our incredible personal power as we are now. As our understanding of human consciousness expands, we are learning more and more about our inherent ability to mold our lives and achieve whatever result we desire. If you choose to tap into this power, you will enhance your own life, and also the lives of others.

Like Attracts Like

Here's the best part: Even if you've failed before, that's okay! Failure is a normal part of life and is often a stepping stone to success. In fact, you'd be hard-pressed to find a highly successful person who hasn't actually had more failures than successes.

- Thomas Edison, a well-known inventor, had thousands of unsuccessful attempts at inventing the light bulb.
- Winston Churchill lost every election for public office until he became Prime Minister at the ripe old age of 62.
- Baseball legend Babe Ruth hit 714 home runs but also struck out 1,330 times in his career.
- English crime novelist John Creasey received 753 rejection slips before he published 564 books.
- Colonel Sanders was rejected over 1,000 times before finally getting funding for his first franchise for KFC (Kentucky Fried Chicken).

An Enlightened Thought for Reflection

I've missed more than 9,000 shots in my career. I've lost almost 300 games. 26 times, I've been trusted to take the game-winning shot and missed. I have failed over and over and over again in my life. And that is why I succeed.

~ Michael Jordan

Your past failures don't dictate your future, nor do they dictate your potential. Your potential is limitless! You can achieve great things by developing this potential and becoming a master of your fate rather than a victim of your circumstances.

Each person's fundamental life goal is to realize their divine nature. All other achievements pale in comparison to understanding your true nature. With self-realization, we become one with Universal Consciousness. Unfortunately, humans are more focused on conquering the external world, including exploring the farthest reaches of space, than they are on understanding their internal world. Lasting happiness can only be achieved by transforming your internal world.

As Aristotle once said, the ultimate goal or purpose of human life is to achieve personal happiness. When we are happy, we are truly enjoying life. We are doing the things we love and sharing that happiness with those around us. When we are happy, our every thought and our every action are coming from a positive and liberating place. If you look at it closely, true and lasting happiness comes when you are growing as a person and, at the same time, contributing to the world around you – thus becoming more God-like in nature. Mother Teresa's greatest joy was to give joy to others!

Life isn't about what you can acquire; it's about what you can become. Your job in this life is to become all that you can be – to push the boundaries of your potential and continue to grow until the day you die; to take on that next goal and take a shot at that bigger dream. This is the purpose of life. This is a purposeful life. This is a life worth living – with "juice," gusto, and passion!

At age 25, business legend Jim Rohn was advised by his mentor to become a millionaire – but not for the obvious reasons:

> *Do it for the skills you have to learn and the person you have to become. Do it for what you'll end up knowing about the marketplace; what you'll learn about the management of time and working with people.*

Do it for the ability of discovering how to keep your ego in check. For what you have to learn about being benevolent. Being kind as well as being strong. What you have to learn about society and business and government and taxes and becoming an accomplished person to reach the status of millionaire.

All that you have learned and all that you've become to reach the status of millionaire is what's valuable. Not the million dollars.

Let's face it: life is tough. But within the trials and tribulations of life, there are opportunities to learn and develop. Living a life of purpose isn't for the weak-willed. It's about having a goal, something bigger than you, something that propels you out of bed in the morning. Having a purpose lights a fire in your belly – it's the engine that drives all great achievements.

As Within, So Without

Being successful in life is about self-mastery. It's about transforming yourself from the inside out. It's often said that if you don't go within, 'you go without.' This means that if you don't access the amazing power inside you, you'll go without the many things you desire.

We live and operate in the context of two worlds: the world within and the world without. They are not two separate entities, but rather two elements of the same essence. The world within is intangible because it is mental and spiritual. The world without is material and physical. Both have shaped your destiny and will continue to do so for the rest of your life. But here's the *key*: It is the world within that creates the world without. The world within is the *cause*; the world without is the *effect*.

The inner world – your thoughts, beliefs, emotions, and attitudes – is the true source of your power. The outer world – your circumstances, environment, and experiences – is a reflection of the inner world. To transform your outer reality, you must first transform your inner world. For example: If you are facing financial challenges, the lack of money is not the problem. It's a symptom of what's happening internally. The quickest and most effective way to permanently change your financial situation externally is to first change your mindset and thoughts internally.

This inner world or inner being is who you really are and, as such, is imbued with God-like qualities. By connecting with your inner being, you can transform your life and become extraordinary. It's your responsibility to use your inner power for your own good and the good of others.

You Are a Living Magnet

James Allen states:

People do not attract that which they want, but that which they are.

This quote is unmistakably the most profound success quote we have ever come across, period! It encapsulates the essence of the Law of Attraction. Understand it. Internalize it. It's the cornerstone upon which this book is built.

At first glance, it may seem simple: what you possess reflects who you are based on your profession or personality. This is mostly true. However, there is a deeper meaning in this statement that may not be immediately apparent. According to James Allen, people attract what they *are*. Therefore, the question should not be, "Who are you?" but rather, "What are you?" The answer is: You are a force of nature – *a living, breathing magnet!*

Let us elaborate on this incredible realization.

Remember our atom analogy? Everything is energy. You are simply a unique bundle of conscious, living energy that creates your individual consciousness, which, in turn, is an infinitesimal yet integral part of Universal Consciousness.

Through the science of quantum physics, we have come to understand that, as individuals, we are a composite of particles vibrating at a particular frequency. Our own unique frequency discerns and separates us from the vibrational frequency of other people and objects. In essence, we are *vibrational* beings.

As a living organism, you are a living magnet. You have electric and magnetic properties. Your entire body is a field of electromagnetic energy. You are a powerhouse of magnetic energy. As such, you have an incredible power of attraction.

One of the most basic principles of the Law of Attraction is the attraction of similarities. This means that the energy you give off will draw in similar energy. Like attracts like – you attract the things with which you resonate. Your thoughts and emotions are potent instruments in the Law of Attraction. They create your reality.

Whatever you want, wants you. Whatever you are moving towards, is moving towards you. The more aligned you are with the things you want, the more easily you attract them. By *purposely* selecting positive thoughts and nurturing positive emotions, you turn yourself into a living magnet for the life you want. This is effectively how you invoke the Law of Attraction.

You Can Change the World

Dr. David R. Hawkins (M.D., Ph.D.), a renowned pioneer in consciousness research and spirituality, has dedicated decades to studying human consciousness and its impact on the world. In his book "The Eye of the I" (2001), he explains how he developed a scale, using kinesiology techniques, to measure individual consciousness levels. This scale ranges from 1 (barely alive) to 1000 (enlightenment).

Dr. Hawkins found that 87% of the human population has a Consciousness Calibration (CC) below 200, living in states of shame, guilt, weakness, and negativity. However, a small percentage of individuals operate at higher levels, radiating positive energy that can counterbalance the negativity of countless others. Here's a breakdown:

- One person who lives in a state of optimism with a willingness to be non-judgmental of others will counterbalance the negativity of 90,000 individuals who calibrate at the lower energy levels.
- One person who lives in a state of pure love and reverence for all life will counterbalance the negativity of 750,000 individuals who calibrate at lower energy levels.
- One person who lives in a state of illumination, bliss, and infinite peace will counterbalance the negativity of 10 million people who calibrate at the lower energy levels (approximately 22 such sages are alive today).
- One person who lives from a state of grace, pure spirit beyond the body, in a world of non-duality or complete oneness, will counterbalance the negativity of 70 million people who calibrate at the lower energy levels (approximately 10 such sages are alive today).

Finally, Dr. Hawkins suggested that one single avatar who can be given the title of Lord (such as Lord Krishna, Lord Jesus, and Lord Buddha) would counterbalance the collective negativity of all of humankind in today's world. The negativity of the entire human population would self-destruct were it not for the counteracting effects of these higher energy fields. (Dyer, 2011)

This means that you have the power to change your life – and, indeed, to change the world. By elevating your consciousness and living in a state of optimism, love, and reverence for all life, you, too, can counterbalance the negativity of many thousands of people.

As you move forward on this journey of self-discovery, carry with you this empowering knowledge. Live purposefully – embrace your divine nature, tap into your inner power, and align yourself with the infinite potential of the universe.

Living purposefully is about using your rare gifts and talents to fulfill that specific role that only you can perform. You can choose whether to live your life with intent and purpose, or let yourself drift through your days with a lack of passion and achievement. Most people drift through life without ever discovering why they are here, or their special calling or purpose. Don't let this be you. Let the words of Florence Scovel Shinn inspire you to pursue your special calling in life:

> *There is, for each man [or woman], perfect self-expression. There is a place which he is to fill, and no one else can fill, something which he is to do, which no one else can do; it is his destiny!*
>
> ~ Florence Scovel Shinn, The Game of Life and How to Play It (2004)

Just consider how much better the world would be if more people lived at higher levels of consciousness. The positive energy from everyone would transform our planet into a more harmonious and prosperous world for everyone.

In the following chapters, we'll explore practical ways to harness your magnetic power, align your thoughts, emotions, and actions with your deepest desires, and unlock the secrets to living a purposeful life.

Hidden truths:

1. You are divine. Your soul is the individualized essence of God.
2. You operate from two worlds. It is the world within that creates the world without.
3. 'People do not attract that which they want, but that which they *are*.'
4. You are a vibrational being. By vibrating at a higher level of consciousness, you counteract the collective negativity of thousands of others.

Chapter 4

Your Greatest Challenge – It's Easier to Conquer Than You Think

Do you yearn for greater happiness, prosperity, meaning, and satisfaction in life? Of course, you do. Such a quest demands significant change, which must originate from within. This is the essence of self-improvement – the willingness to transform oneself from the inside out.

Most people desire an enriched and fulfilling life, yet they shy away from the work of self-improvement. To use an analogy, they aspire to build skyscrapers but avoid laying the proper foundations. Instead, they conform to social norms, seeking quick fixes and shortcuts to success. Unfortunately, such shortcuts don't exist. It's by thinking outside the box and stepping beyond social norms (or standards) that we make new discoveries and progress.

Life is about growth, and growth means change. Change can be tough, but resisting it is tougher. Resisting growth denies you success. True success demands a willingness to make sacrifices, face challenges, and learn from every experience. Also, the bigger your goals, the more you need to grow.

An Enlightened Thought for Reflection

*Life is a series of experiences, each one of which makes us bigger...
for the world was built to develop character, and we must learn that
the setbacks and griefs we endure help us in our marching onward.*

~ Henry Ford

Success is not a one-time accomplishment, such as graduating from college or purchasing a home. It's an exciting, ever-changing journey. To achieve greater success, you need to increase your value. The more valuable you are to others, the more they will want to connect with you. To live a successful life, increase your value, then express that value through contribution to the betterment of others.

Success belongs to those who continually learn more, who develop an ongoing learning capability and exploit it. True wealth, or true abundance in life, comes only after you stop focusing on the money and start focusing on doing something that's going to improve you personally.

As Alvin Toffler so eloquently put it:

The illiterate of the 21st century will not be those who cannot read and write, but those who cannot learn, unlearn and relearn.

When you taste success, it motivates you to aim higher because you realize you have the potential to do more. With each achievement, you begin to operate from a new and higher level. Every accomplishment lifts you up to a new height, pushing you to set larger targets. We have an insatiable desire to achieve and fulfill our true purpose in life. Such is our nature.

To achieve a certain outcome, you need to be in vibrational resonance with the outcome you want to manifest. Your desire for that outcome will automatically attract opportunities, often disguised as unassailable challenges. These challenges enable you to develop in capability and reap the rewards of your labor.

Develop a Success Mindset

The mindset of successful people is distinct from others. They think and act differently. They consistently defy conformity, doing things that others will not do to achieve results that others believe they cannot. What seems like the right thing to do for most people is actually not the norm for the top 1%. To be the best, it is imperative to go against the grain of conventional wisdom.

To create a new reality, reinvent yourself. It's not possible to change your current life with the same thinking that created it. As Albert Einstein famously said:

> We cannot solve our problems with the same level of thinking that created them.

Let go of the mindset that created your current situation to open the way for a mindset that breeds success. Achieving success in life hinges on shifting your mindset from one of powerlessness to one of true power.

To start this shift, you need to change from:

- Thinking about lack and limited supply to thinking about abundance and unlimited supply.
- Short-term, immediate gratification thinking to long-term, delayed-gratification thinking.
- Win-lose thinking to win-win thinking.
- Security thinking to opportunity thinking.
- Survival consciousness to prosperity consciousness.
- Competing and cloning to collaborating and creating.
- Focusing on getting to focusing on giving.

- Making an impression to making a difference.

Throughout history, the strong-willed have tried to dominate and impose their views on life onto others. The submissive type is taught to fit in, adapt, and conform – to go along to get along. It may seem easier to adapt to their ideas of what is best for you rather than work things out yourself. However, meekly or forcibly accepting the ideas of others can seriously disadvantage you – suppress your individuality, hamper your progress, and stunt your growth.

While it is important to learn from the accumulated wisdom of others as you evolve and grow, your instincts may tell you to tread a unique path. It's a choice only you can make, whether to take the beaten trail or follow your instincts – and there's nothing more exciting!

If you're feeling frustrated with your life, it's likely that you have relinquished your freedom to consciously create your own life experiences, the very things that eventually bring you joy. Often, a frustrated life means you've chosen the path of least resistance and effectively become stuck. To move forward, it's necessary to get 'unstuck.'

Each of us has our personal desires or goals. Achieving these goals generates deep personal happiness. When we fail to embrace our true passions, it becomes harder to find genuine, lasting success. Success comes faster when we do the things we enjoy and *want* to do. Doing the things that give us no personal satisfaction is exhausting, demotivating, and soul-destroying.

When you consider the many elements that have influenced and shaped your current reality, you may realize that there is much to undo and reprogram. However, when you understand your divine nature and the unfaltering natural Laws of the Universe, you see that everything you've done has brought you to this point; you can now consciously choose more empowering thoughts and actions. This realization releases you from a victim mentality. Understanding how your past created your present empowers you to recreate your future by confronting your greatest challenge – your comfort zone!

Your Comfort Zone

The average person has dreams and aspirations for a better life, usually involving lifestyle and material objects. As we grow older and wiser, we may realize that there is more to life than material wealth. Finding purpose and meaning in life will eventually become the primary goal.

If you are 'normal,' you have a comfort zone, generally considered a mental rather than a physical space. A reserved person will find it uncomfortable to start a conversation with a stranger, or someone afraid of snakes might not want to go on an Australian bushwalk in summer. There are countless behaviors that thwart success in life by imprisoning you in your comfort zone.

As you move towards your goals, your comfort zone will challenge you every step of the way. It's just the Universe's way of *preparing* you to receive your desired outcome. Therefore, it's important that you understand and master the concept of the comfort zone. Let's use the diagram below to examine how this can affect your life.

Figure 4.1

The innermost circle represents you at a particular point in time. The outer concentric circles depict your growth and expansion over time. As the diagram shows, your dreams lie outside your comfort zone!

We are programmed to operate within our comfort zone, which acts as a protective barrier. It supposedly keeps us safe, signaling danger when we engage in unfamiliar behaviors like walking along the edge of a cliff without safety barriers. While it serves a very useful purpose, it also quickly outlives its usefulness by stifling growth and progress.

Humans are creatures of habit, but achieving your goals demands that you become more than you are now. This requires you to push and expand the boundary of your comfort zone, thereby growing in 'consciousness' – the circle becomes a bit larger (as shown by the progressively expanding circle in Figure 4.1). It means doing things that you would not normally do, even taking risks or doing things that might make you look clumsy or foolish. It's precisely at these challenging moments where real growth takes place. Progress in life requires that you constantly confront and overcome challenging situations.

If you just wish and passively wait, your goals and dreams will fail to materialize. The key is to keep growing and expanding until you encompass your dreams, as depicted by the outermost circle in the diagram. You will then grow in consciousness to a level that resonates and matches with your dreams. (Take note of the expanding circle as it is an integral part of the Success Continuum® introduced in the next chapter.)

Goals push us towards new behaviors we'd rather avoid. Usually, this requires abandoning old behaviors and adopting new ones. This can be quite a challenge for most people, and it is one of the main reasons people don't achieve their goals.

Having a goal is actually a *planned conflict* with the comfort zone.

It means leaving the familiar surroundings of the comfort zone and exploring new territory. Sometimes exploring new territory can be exciting. Quite often, it is daunting because you don't want to leave the safety of your comfort zone. To reach any significant goal, you must leave your comfort zone.

Pushing through your comfort zone takes conscious effort and some risk. The inducement for staying in your comfort zone is that you don't have to put in extra effort or take risks. Regrettably, the consequence of not pushing the boundaries of your comfort zone is that you never achieve your dreams. Understand that your dreams don't come to you; you must grow and expand until you encompass your dreams.

The comfort zone may be pushed gently or hard – you choose. However, the manner in which you push through your comfort zone will determine how quickly you grow and, therefore, how quickly you will achieve your desired outcome in life.

Virend overcame asthma through sheer tenacity by constantly pushing the boundaries of his comfort zone. Here is his story:

Beating Asthma

As a child, I had chronic asthma. When I was about five or six, I overheard my grandmother saying to my mother, "I don't know how long this child will live."

Born and raised in South Africa during the apartheid era, I was fortunate to live near one of the four public swimming pools built for people of Indian origin. The pool was about half the size of an Olympic pool.

During peak periods, the pool was overcrowded, with literally no room to swim anywhere except in the deep end because not everyone was an adept swimmer. So, if you could swim a few strokes, it was better to venture into the deep end.

Initially, I could only swim two or three strokes before gasping for air. As there was no room to practice in the shallow end, I decided to do what some other kids did: hold tightly onto the railing, go to the far corner of the deep end, and then swim diagonally across the corner from one wall to the other.

As an asthmatic capable of swimming only three strokes, colliding with another swimmer was a serious threat. People who could swim confidently jumped into the pool almost anywhere, often obstructing my path.

Forced to extend my limits, I'd swallow water while desperately trying to reach the pool's edge. The pool superintendent would sometimes catch me out and send me back to the shallow end, where I belonged.

Despite this, I loved the pool. I often stayed until early evening, when the pool was quieter, to practice my strokes.

Gradually, I could swim four or five strokes comfortably. As summers passed, my swimming improved. Whenever I reached my limit, I'd tell myself, "One more." This became my mantra. Even exhausted, I'd push myself to beat my previous best. Slowly but surely, I progressed from five to six to seven strokes, eventually completing a full lap without stopping.

Of course, I did not stop there. I kept pushing the boundaries of my comfort zone. I became a very strong swimmer, and in my teens, I swam competitively and even qualified as a surf lifesaver.

My tenacity and asthma did not get along. As I developed my stamina and lung capacity, my asthma became weaker and weaker. Eventually, my asthma could no longer deal with my inner strength, and it left for good!

Do What It Takes

Realize that you are capable of much more than you are demonstrating. It's true, not just positive thinking. But it takes an enormous amount of effort to push yourself to the limit… and simply reaching your limit is not good enough. You must dig deeper. If you want to get better, you must push past your limits, doing more than you *think* you can. This is where the real growth occurs. Don't simply do your best; do what it *takes*. There is a major difference between doing your best and doing what it *takes* to reach your goal.

Our capacity to accomplish is only a state of mind. How much we can do depends on how much we *think* we can do. You have the capacity within you to achieve just about any outcome you set for yourself, but you have to grow to manifest that outcome. Growing requires that you challenge yourself and endure prolonged periods of discomfort. But, the end will justify the means; the rewards will be worth it.

Every person we know who has the ability to live life on their own terms has consistently pushed the boundaries of their comfort zone, accepting full responsibility for their own success. The concept of the comfort zone is beautifully illustrated in the following poem.

The Comfort Zone

I used to have a comfort zone where I knew I wouldn't fail.
The same four walls and busywork were really more like jail.
I longed so much to do the things I'd never done before,
But stayed inside my comfort zone and paced the same old floor.

I said it didn't matter that I wasn't doing much.
I said I didn't care for things like commission checks and such.
I claimed to be so busy with things inside my zone,
But deep inside I longed for something special of my own.

I couldn't let my life go by just watching others win.
I held my breath; I stepped outside and let the change begin.
I took a step and with new strength I'd never felt before,
I kissed my comfort zone goodbye and closed and locked
the door.

If you're in a comfort zone, afraid to venture out,
Remember that all winners were at one time filled with doubt.
A step or two and words of praise can make your dreams
come true.
Reach for your future with a smile; success is there for you!

~ Anonymous

Each of us has two natures: one that wants to move forward and another
that wants to pull back. As we experience life, one of these natures will
dominate.

It is your choice as to which nature will dominate.

As we conclude this transformative chapter, contemplate the profound
challenge that lies before you: the conquest of your comfort zone. This is
not just a trivial obstacle but the key to releasing your true potential and
achieving the success you desire.

Remember, your comfort zone is not a physical space but a mental
construct – a self-imposed limitation that you have the power to
overcome. Every time you push beyond its boundaries, you grow,
evolve, and move closer to your dreams.

The journey of self-improvement may seem daunting, but it is the most
rewarding path you can embark upon. It's not about changing who you
are at your core, but about becoming the best version of yourself – the
version capable of achieving your wildest dreams.

As you move forward, realize that discomfort is not your enemy but your ally in growth. Embrace the challenges that lie ahead, for they are the stepping stones to your success. Your greatest achievements await you just beyond the edge of your comfort zone.

In the following chapters, we'll explore practical strategies for consistently expanding your comfort zone, aligning your actions with your aspirations, and transforming your potential into tangible success. Your journey of personal growth and extraordinary achievement begins with the decision to step beyond the familiar and into the world of unlimited possibility.

Are you ready?

Hidden truths:

1. True wealth, or abundance in life, comes only *after* you stop focusing on the money and start focusing on doing something that's going to improve you personally.
2. To achieve a certain outcome, you need to be in vibrational resonance with the outcome you want to manifest.
3. Your dreams lie *outside* your comfort zone.
4. To reach any significant goal, you must leave your comfort zone, push past your limits, and do more than you think you can.

Chapter 5

Unlock the Secrets to True Prosperity

Picture a life where every day is filled with purpose, joy, and a deep sense of satisfaction. This isn't wishful thinking; it's the reality of true prosperity. But achieving this state requires more than just amassing wealth – it's about advancing personal growth and making meaningful contributions to the world around you.

Let's take a step back and really think about what it means to live a prosperous life. When you hear the word *prosperity*, what pops into your head? For many, it's an image of luxury and opulence – a life overflowing with material possessions. But true prosperity is so much more. It's the freedom to pursue what truly brings you joy, the vigor to live each day to the fullest, and the means to give generously to others. It's a force that touches every part of your life, way beyond your finances.

This perspective often raises thoughtful questions from those who observe that material success doesn't always correspond with personal growth. We see examples of wealthy individuals who operate from a place of ego and self-interest, while many deeply conscious and giving individuals – artists, teachers, healers – may not achieve comparable material wealth.

But here's the truth: external prosperity alone is an incomplete measure of success – having *things* doesn't mean you have *everything*. Many people with all the external markers of success – money, prestige, influence – privately struggle with stress, broken relationships, or a nagging sense of emptiness. The millionaire who can't sleep at night or the CEO battling constant anxiety show us that wealth alone doesn't guarantee fulfillment.

Now, real prosperity? That requires the courage to step beyond your comfort zone. Whether you're an entrepreneur risking capital or an artist sharing vulnerable work with the world, meaningful success demands facing fear and uncertainty. Those who choose the apparent safety of conformity often trade their deeper aspirations for predictability.

And here's the thing – prosperity isn't always measured in financial terms. A teacher who inspires, an artist who stirs emotions, a monk who finds deep peace – aren't they *rich* in a different, perhaps even more meaningful way? Their success lies in their impact and personal fulfillment, doing what they were meant to do, rather than their bank balance.

All said, prosperity isn't some end goal you reach and check off – it's a journey of continuous growth and contribution. It's about seeing opportunities rather than limitations and recognizing that there are many paths to fulfillment. When we adopt this perspective, we discover new ways to create value and experience joy – whether through business, creativity, service to others, or personal development.

At its core, prosperity comes down to a simple formula:

Prosperity = Growth + Contribution

This equation is the foundation for an extraordinary life. Personal growth and contribution are not separate journeys; they are deeply interconnected. As you grow personally, you increase your capacity to contribute meaningfully to others, creating a cycle of fulfillment that enriches your life and those around you.

Let's examine how applying this formula can optimize your potential.

Growth: The Catalyst for Your Future

Personal growth is the catalyst for prosperity. It's about realizing the best version of yourself, not just for your benefit but for the greater good. Consider growth an investment in your future self – one that yields rewards in purpose and achievement.

As you improve, so do your circumstances. In other words, your situation can only improve to the extent that you improve.

To grow in affluence, it's essential to grow in intelligence and wisdom. Many people desire prosperity but never attain it because they lack the character traits that qualify them for such a life. To attract abundance, first develop the qualities of an abundant person.

Lifelong learning is necessary for prosperity in our rapidly changing world. As your wisdom expands, so does your ability to create value.

Now let's look at contribution, the second essential component of the formula.

Contribution: Your Purpose in Action

Contribution is how your personal growth manifests itself in the world. It's about sharing your special talents to uplift others. When you make a difference, you help others and inspire your sense of purpose.

We all have something unique and valuable to offer. Yours might be teaching, creating art, helping others in need, or creating new solutions. Find your passions, apply your strengths, and uplift those around you. Adding value to others' lives will profoundly transform your own, leaving you feeling more connected, valued, and energized.

Prosperity stems from operating at a higher level of understanding – an understanding that rewards follow service and that service (or duty) is not a chore, but a privilege. Even small acts can have significant ripple effects when done with good intentions.

As the great poet and India's first Nobel laureate, Rabindranath Tagore, so eloquently put it:

I slept and dreamt that life was joy;
I awoke and found that life was duty;
I acted, and behold!
Duty was joy.

Let there be no illusions about what it takes to be happy and prosperous – the connection between personal growth and contribution is the key to unlocking your true potential. When you concentrate on improving yourself and aiding others, prosperity inevitably ensues.

Prosperity is an Effect

Prosperity is an *effect* (or outcome), and there is an underlying *cause* for every effect. The Success Continuum® exemplifies this, showing prosperity depends on growth and contribution.

Success Continuum ®

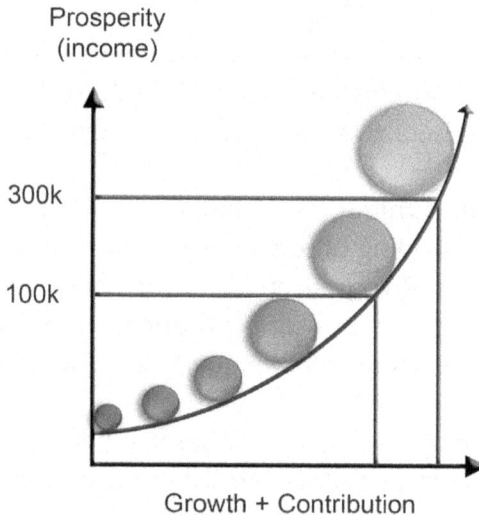

Figure 5.1

The Success Continuum® maps the equation: Prosperity = Growth + Contribution

It's a basic graph relating personal growth and societal contribution (the x-axis) to prosperity (the y-axis). The curved line on the graph represents your personal learning or growth curve (the "continuum"), which is endless – there is no end to how much you can learn, grow, and succeed.

The expanding circles represent your evolution through challenging comfort zones (as illustrated in Figure 4.1). Your position on the curve reflects your consciousness level at any point in life. Understanding your location is essential for gauging your prosperity level. Expressed in financial terms, income depends on growth and societal contributions.

The more valuable you become, the more opportunities you can seize and earn income. Rabindranath Tagore perfectly sums up the concept of receiving value by *becoming* valuable:

> *Everything comes to us that belongs to us if we create the capacity to receive it.*

Currently, wherever you are on the curve is your maximum prosperity level. Your responsibility is to determine where you are and where you want to be in the future.

Although prosperity encompasses more than money, let's use income to demonstrate. If you currently earn $100,000 annually ($100k) but desire $300k, that's a significant gap requiring concrete steps to close through personal growth and societal contribution.

The simple truth is that your income will only grow to the extent that you do. You can't attract and maintain more than your consciousness permits. For example, if you have what I call a "$35,000 mindset," that is all you will attract or maintain. This explains the common phenomenon of lottery winners going broke – their mindset hasn't expanded to match their newfound wealth.

If we were to distribute all the money in the world equally among every man, woman, and child, a significantly uneven distribution would soon emerge. Most of the money would end up in the hands of those with a mindset focused on prosperity. As bestselling author Harvey MacKay noted:

> *When a person with money meets a person with experience, the person with the experience winds up with the money, and the person with the money winds up with the experience.*

Consciousness Creates Reality

Your experience of life matches your level of prosperity consciousness. By accumulating experiences, you automatically raise your level of consciousness. *Consciousness creates reality!*

The Success Continuum depicts various levels of consciousness. As vibrating energy, your external world reflects internal vibrations. Negative emotions – fears, doubts, uncertainties, resentments, jealousy, etc. – lower your frequency and may cause temporary slides backward. Positive emotions raise it. You can change frequencies, shifting your position on the curve.

As you give off better vibes and grow in consciousness, you expand outward in all directions and move upwards along the continuum toward a higher state of being, eventually to a state characterized by increased awareness, compassion, and love.

Consciously ascending the continuum means going on a spiritual path. Deepak Chopra reminds us that:

> *We are not human beings who have occasional spiritual experiences. We are actually spiritual beings who have (occasional) human experiences.*

Your world and experiences are a direct reflection of your vibrational state. If you want to know at what level you have been vibrating, look at your life. You are a product of your past thoughts and behaviors.

If you don't already have what you want, you have chosen to limit your growth and contribution, expressing your identity at a lower vibrational frequency than your target goal. Your vibration, therefore, does not match the vibration of your desire.

Overcome negative emotions that are inhibiting your upward movement. Realize that external factors don't limit you – consciousness does. You can uplift your state at any time.

The absolute truth is that you will never achieve sustainable success that exceeds your level of consciousness. What you become matters more than what you get, determining your results. Embody the consciousness level you desire. In this embodiment lies the secret to true prosperity.

Upcoming chapters provide strategies to raise consciousness, align vibrations to your goals, and transform your potential into tangible prosperity.

Your journey continues. Prosperity awaits!

Hidden truths:

1.   You choose the level of consciousness at which you wish to express your identity.
2.   You cannot attract more than the level of your consciousness.
3.   Consciousness equates to reality!
4.   What you become will determine what you get.

Chapter 6

The Stuff that Dreams Are Really Made Of

The Evolution of Consciousness

A profound shift is occurring in human consciousness. We are seeing new levels of awareness and creativity, fueled by the realization that:

- the universe is made up entirely of energy, and
- our thoughts have the power to shape this energy into our reality.

This represents a progressive leap in collective consciousness – millions are uncovering their innate ability to create the lives of their dreams. Quantum physics validates this perspective, revealing that our *observations* bring all things in our world into being. In essence, our thoughts translate energy into the experiences we call reality. Let's examine the implications of this game-changing insight.

Decoding the Energy Around Us

Everything, including ourselves, is composed of subatomic particles – waves of energy vibrating at specific frequencies. This electromagnetic energy originates from Universal Consciousness and emanates as light, which is everywhere, all around you and within you. You can't see this light unless it is reflected or refracted off some medium. You think that you see with your eyes, but it is really *your mind* that sees.

Your eyes don't see anything at all, just as a camera lens does not see anything because they don't have the consciousness to interpret what they're detecting. They detect and focus light. Effectively, your eyes are sensory organs that receive the electromagnetic vibrations of light and transmit them to your conscious mind for interpretation as a perceived pattern of shapes, colors, and textures. In other words, your eyes are sensory gateways, gathering light waves for your mind to interpret as images.

When you gaze at your hand, what you're actually seeing is light bouncing off the electromagnetic energy that makes up the substance of your hand. Before you put your focus to it, your hand was simply unseen energy. It takes on the appearance of your hand the moment you observe it. This suggests that subatomic particles that make up your hand (or anything else for that matter) "come into existence" only when you think about them!

Consider the film The Matrix – the character Neo could shape reality at will by thoughts alone. While fictional, it mirrors a profound truth – our world originates from dynamic, responsive energy, which we can reshape with focused minds to influence the world around us.

It's a game-changing realization. Imagine having the power to shape your destiny and create the future you dream about. The truth is, you're not just a passive observer in your life – you're the architect or creator. Your thoughts are the building blocks of your reality, and *every moment*, you're constructing the life you're living!

Change Your Thinking, Change Your Life

Think about it: your thoughts are the sum total of who you are, and since you're the one doing the thinking, you're 100% accountable for the results you're getting. It's a staggering responsibility but also an incredible opportunity. When you realize that your thoughts are the key to releasing your potential, you can start to make deliberate choices that transform your life. Put simply, if you change your thinking, you change your life!

The more you understand how your thoughts create your life experiences, the more powerful you will become as a creator of your own reality. When you allow others to constantly impose their views or beliefs upon you, you give up your control to shape your life. This means that others are shaping your future for you. But this does not mean we can then shift the blame for our undesirable results to others. Understand that you can give up your control, but you cannot give up your responsibility. The power to choose is vested in you. Therefore, you are always responsible for your outcomes in life, favorable or unfavorable. It is up to you to take conscious and deliberate control of your thoughts to shape your own destiny.

Most people have heard about thought and its creative power, but only a few really understand this concept. If a thought is so powerful that it can actually shape your destiny, doesn't it make sense to understand *exactly* what it is?

Picture what a thought might look like. What are the defining features?

Take a moment now, and mentally or physically (if you have a pen and paper), draw a picture of a thought with its essential characteristics.

Thoughts Are "Things!"

Fact: Thoughts are actual things – *real* things!

Thoughts

Figure 6.1

Thoughts are like energy waves, each with its own frequency and strength. Like radio waves, thoughts go out into the universe and attract complementary vibrations or waves of energy that are in harmony with them.

All things are created *mentally* first, and then they are created physically. The basis of all creation is thought. First, you have them, and then they "have" you because they become part of who you are, guiding your actions and creating your reality – you act in a manner consistent with your thinking. In other words, you are the product of your dominant thoughts.

When you think or speak a thought, the energy or vibration of that thought or word goes out into the universe. It then attracts a similar vibration and brings it back into the constantly changing energy field that surrounds you, reflecting your inner state, intentions, and focus.

Although all thought is creative, you are unlikely to instantly attract the exact thing you thought about. Instead, you attract into your energy orbit the people, circumstances, events, opportunities, and resources needed to turn that thought into reality. So, your thoughts ultimately translate into physical things either by default or by design. If it is by design, then you are actively shaping your outcomes by being a co-creator with the Universe.

Often, we are told that to change our results in life, we must develop new behaviors. The truth is that we cannot change anything in our lives without first changing the originating cause – our thoughts. This is a massive shift in perspective!

The Stuff that Dreams Are Really Made Of

Internationally renowned author and speaker Dr. Wayne Dyer writes:

> *...all of our behavior results from the thoughts that preceded it... so the thing to work on is not your behavior but the thing that caused your behavior, your thoughts.*

Take a moment to notice the world you have created around you. It is the sum total of your thoughts. If you have been thinking in terms of lack (or deficiency), if that is your dominant vibration, then that is what you have been attracting. Conversely, if you have consistently been thinking of abundance, you would be attracting the circumstances to manifest abundance.

Here is one of our favorite excerpts:

> *There is a thinking stuff from which all things are made, and which, in its original state, permeates, penetrates and fills the interspaces of the universe. A thought in this substance produces the thing imaged by the thought. A person can form things in his thought, and by impressing his thought upon formless substance, can cause the thing he thinks about to be created. (Wattles, 2002)*

To paraphrase this quote: everything in existence is made from the same stuff – *thinking stuff*. This stuff is found everywhere there appears to be empty space – it *permeates, penetrates, and fills the interspaces of the universe*. But, as we know, there is really no empty space because the space is filled with this invisible thinking stuff, which we know as thoughts. This is the very stuff that dreams are made of – *literally*! When you think about something, the mental image of the thing you think about is converted into a vibration and sent into this *formless substance*, where it meets other thoughts that are in harmony with it. (Formless means that the substance has not taken form or shape yet.) And, if you consistently *impress* this same thought upon the formless substance, you will cause it to take shape and be *created* in its physical form.

You've probably heard the phrase, "What you think about, you bring about." This is not entirely true – it's not just the thinking that matters.

If thoughts lack emotional intensity, they will have little or no effect – they're like fireworks without a spark. *Emotion* or feeling is the critical element of the manifestation process.

That's why, when you simply *have to have* something, that raw emotion kicks in. It's like turning up the volume on your thoughts – the emotion amplifies their vibration to make them resonate louder and clearer in the universe. And the more intense your thoughts, the quicker things start falling into place. It's less about hoping and more about *feeling* it into being.

So *thought* is the cause, *form* is the effect, and *emotion* is the accelerator in the process of manifestation!

David Ramsey talks about people taking control of their financial future as having a *focused intensity* and *getting mad* about change. He says:

> They got sick and tired of being sick and tired! They said, 'I've had it!' and went ballistic to change their lives. There is no intellectual exercise where you can academically work your way into wealth; you have to get fired up. There is no energy in logic... this is behavior and motivation modification, and it works! (Ramsey, 2003)

Your feelings reflect your emotional state. It is most important to elicit the emotion. E-motion is energy in motion – call it 'emotionalized energy.' Emotion is the power that attracts. Emotion is the language of the Universe. Remember, emotion is the language you use to talk to God. Fear and desire are two of your strongest emotions. That which you fear or desire strongly, you *will* experience.

Examples from Life

One of our acquaintances lost all his belongings due to bankruptcy. He couldn't find a regular job and had to work from home. He needed a car to meet his clients. Desperate to get a car, he entered a raffle contest where the first prize was a car. His desire to own the car was so strong that he attracted the experience by winning the contest! It would be fair to say that he was the most emotionally charged participant in the contest.

We also know a wonderful woman who constantly looked at herself in the mirror and worried about the pimples on her face. Not surprisingly, she always had pimples on her face, no matter what she did to treat the problem. It was her fear of having pimples that attracted that experience.

What we emotionally energize, positive or negative, we magnetize... be it a new car, someone scratching the paintwork of your new vehicle, pimples, a virus on your computer, an abusive partner, cancer, or almost anything else.

Maintaining Magnificent Dreams

Sustained energy is required for attraction and creation. A strong intention has an intense emotional energy. When you move emotionally charged energy, you create an effect. When you move enough energy, you create matter – physical form. Matter (physical stuff) is energy conglomerated, moved around, and shoved together to create something tangible. Thought mixed with emotion creates something of physical form.

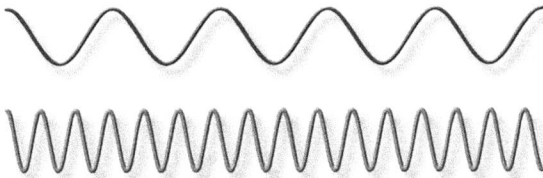

Figure 6.2 Thoughts versus Thoughts mixed with emotion (lower bar)

The more emotion you attach to a thought, the greater its rate of vibration (as shown in Figure 6.2 above) and, therefore, its power of attraction. You will rapidly attract into your life the resources and situations that are in harmony with that thought. Have you noticed that as you increase the strength of your emotions, you become more excited, enthusiastic, convinced, and determined?

When this happens, all your inborn cosmic powers are activated, and you begin to move rapidly towards your goals, and your goals begin to move rapidly towards you. In this elevated state, your goals and resources operate as synchronized magnets, pulling each other into physical form. The reverse is also true when you emit negative emotions.

To clarify, emotion is the accelerator of the manifestation process. The stronger the emotion, the faster the process of manifestation. Your emotional energy can change your vibration to a very high or a very low level *in an instant*! If it changes to a very high frequency, it could quickly give you what you desire or fear.

However, note that just because you manifested a desired outcome does not mean that you will hold onto that outcome indefinitely. Remember, you do not get what you want in life, but you get what you *are*. Sustainable success is something you attract according to the person you become – the vibrational state of your entire being. Maintain the level of consciousness (vibrational state) at which you attracted the desired outcome, and your prosperity will be sustained; otherwise, it will eventually wither away (similar to the fleeting nature of a lottery win).

Your Amazing Subconscious Mind

Did you know that your mind is not your brain? The brain is a physical organ, but the mind is non-physical, a powerful force of vibrating energy. The mind cannot be seen or touched, but it definitely exists. Other than saying the mind is not a physical thing, no one can say for sure how it works.

There's a fascinating story of an organ transplant recipient who took on some of her donor's traits.

Claire, a former professional dancer, was 47 and dying from a disease called primary pulmonary hypertension when, in 1988, she had a pioneering heart-lung transplant in America. After she recovered from the operation, she suddenly had a craving for beer and KFC (Kentucky Fried Chicken). She was baffled because she had never before desired either. According to her teenage daughter, she even began walking like a man.

Months after the operation, she began having mysterious dreams about a young man named Tim. She tracked down the donor of her new organs and learned that they had come from Timothy, the victim of a fatal motorcycle accident. When she contacted his family, the woman was stunned to learn that he did have a particular fondness for drinking beer and eating KFC.

(Sylvia, 2008)

Claire's story is undeniably intriguing. She had a heart-lung transplant, *not* a brain transplant! The story raises the question: Is information stored in every cell of our body and not only in the brain or mind? Regardless, it highlights the fascinating mysteries surrounding the connections between body and mind.

While we know that the mind is not a physical entity, we also know that we possess a conscious and subconscious mind. The conscious mind encompasses all that we are aware of. It is the controlled, intellectual part of the mind that performs everyday work.

In contrast, the subconscious mind encompasses things outside our conscious awareness. Even if we don't always realize it, our subconscious mind is constantly influencing our daily lives. For example, have you ever driven home from work and arrived without remembering how you got there? That's your subconscious mind at work. It takes over routine tasks, so your conscious mind can focus on other things. By understanding and working with our subconscious mind we can develop greater self-awareness, personal growth, and emotional intelligence.

So, what exactly is the *subconscious* mind?

The subconscious mind is a complex and multifaceted concept that plays a critical role in shaping our thoughts, feelings, and behaviors. Given its invisibility, here is an exercise that may clarify its essence: Picture what the subconscious mind would look like if you could illustrate it. Mentally or physically (if you have a pen and paper), draw a picture of the subconscious mind with its essential characteristics.

Perplexing, isn't it?

According to Dr. Maxwell Maltz, the best-selling author of "Psycho-Cybernetics":

> *The new science of 'Cybernetics' has furnished us with convincing proof that the so-called 'subconscious mind' is not a mind at all, but a mechanism – a goal-striving 'servo-mechanism' consisting of the brain and nervous system... and like any other servo-mechanism, it must have a clear-cut goal, objective or 'problem' to work upon. The goals that our own Creative Mechanism seeks to achieve are MENTAL IMAGES, or mental pictures, which we create by the use of the IMAGINATION. (Maltz, 1989)*

When one considers this description, the subconscious mind is literally *your entire being*, which incorporates the brain and nervous system. This description makes sense when we understand that everything in existence is just energy and information – including you. The idea that you (your entire self) are a living magnet or a goal-seeking mechanism capable of achieving amazing things should inspire you to take control of your life through your thoughts, words, and actions to achieve your highest aspirations.

Accordingly, a picture of your subconscious mind is a picture of yourself, complete with brain and nervous system.

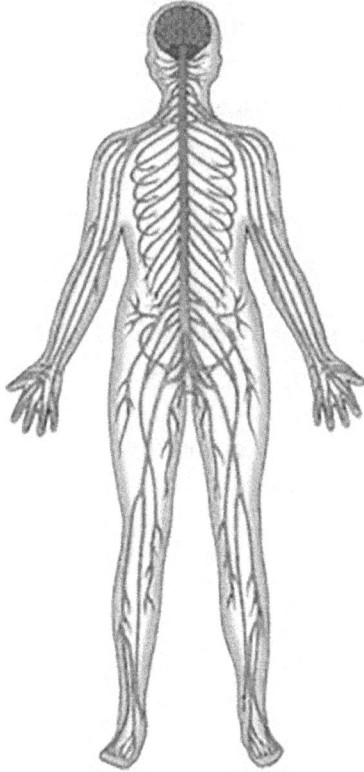

Figure 6.3 – The Subconscious Mind

Effectively, you are a goal-striving servo-mechanism (similar to a heat-seeking missile) capable of achieving almost any goal you set for yourself. As a goal-striving mechanism, when you reach one goal, another will always present itself to you. We all need goals to fulfill our purpose – to grow into all we can be and contribute to making this world better.

As we move forward, take a moment to truly absorb the profound implications of what you've just learned. You are the creator of your own reality. Your thoughts, combined with emotions, form the very foundation upon which your life experiences are built. Your subconscious mind is your entire being – a sophisticated, goal-striving mechanism constantly working to bring your dominant thoughts into reality. It does not differentiate between what you perceive as 'good' or 'bad' – it simply acts on the instructions you provide through your consistent thoughts and feelings.

As you read on, we will uncover practical techniques for utilizing the incredible power of your mind. You will learn how to consciously direct your thoughts, infuse them with the right emotions, and work in harmony with your subconscious to create the life you desire.

Hidden Truths

1. Thought is *cause*, and form is *effect*!
2. Things are created mentally *before* they are created physically – your thoughts eventually become physical things.
3. Emotion is the *accelerator* of the manifestation process.
4. The subconscious mind is your *entire being*, which incorporates the brain and nervous system.
5. The subconscious mind is a *goal-striving servo-mechanism*, making you a living magnet!

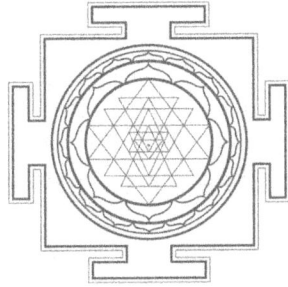

Chapter 7
The Magic of Believing

Throughout life, you develop beliefs that either serve or limit you. "I choose my destiny" is empowering. "I'm a victim" is limiting. Your beliefs are feelings of certainty about something without necessarily being proven. Many beliefs are never questioned, yet they form the basis of how we live our lives and shape our reality.

Believing is Seeing!

Beliefs drive success. Our life experience mirrors our beliefs. By changing our beliefs, we can change our lives.

Many often say, "I'll believe it only when I see it," or "I've got to see it to believe it." They mean they need to see the result before they will believe it is achievable.

But even then, they'll bend what they see to fit their beliefs – gathering proof that life is against them or they're not smart enough. The truth: *believing is seeing*, not seeing is believing. It's a *radically* different concept that very few people comprehend.

First, we must believe; then, we'll see or experience the desired result or outcome. Most people do the opposite, which is why they struggle. Yet the reality is that we see what we believe.

Believe in Yourself and Your Ideas

Two elements of belief are critical to your success in any endeavor:

1. Belief in your dreams and ideas.
2. Belief in yourself.

Unless you genuinely believe in your dreams and ideas, you won't generate the emotion that invokes the Law of Attraction. This law ultimately draws the resources and situations you need to achieve your desired outcome. If you don't believe in yourself and your ability to accomplish your goals, you certainly won't give 100% effort toward achieving them.

When we start a new venture believing that we won't succeed because of temporary setbacks, it's almost guaranteed that we will not succeed. Our beliefs dictate our results! However, if we persist and enjoy even small successes, our beliefs shift, and we start to see what we believe. Franklin D. Roosevelt said,

> *The only limit of our realization of tomorrow will be our doubts of today.*

Doubt keeps us from making long-lasting, positive changes in our lives. Many of us have tiny cracks in our self-image, and when we allow ourselves or others to insert the "wedge of doubt" into those cracks, we set ourselves up for catastrophic failure. The following is a fascinating tale we've adapted to emphasize this point.

The Devil's Best Tool

One day, the devil decided that God had received too much good publicity, and he, too, deserved some acknowledgment for the work he did to make this world an interesting place. He called a major TV news network and, after identifying himself, arranged an interview.

For the interview, he transported the reporter and the camera crew to Hell and gave them a tour of a strange sort of art gallery. His gallery did not consist of elements of great art. Instead, his gallery was made up of a number of rooms of varying sizes, each one dedicated to a specific item of interest. In one room were piles of gold on a marble table, stacked to the ceiling. "This is my greed room," the devil said. "Greed is one of my favorite tools."

Moving to the second room, the devil showed the reporter and camera crew a group of men and women enjoying themselves in a cocktail lounge at a convention. "This is my infidelity room," the devil said. "This is a place of temptation for those who are far away from home."

The devil continued in this manner, proudly presenting rooms with addictive drugs, alcohol, firearms, weapons, and other destructive items.

Finally, the camera crew came to the last room. The devil paused and said, "Herein lies my greatest tool. With this tool, I can accomplish more evil than with all the other tools at my disposal, put together."

Keen to see the contents of this room, the camera crew and the reporter moved closer to the door as the devil opened it triumphantly. In the room was a small item on a pedestal illuminated by a spotlight.

At first glance, it appeared to be a seemingly harmless wedge-shaped object. Curiously, the camera crew edged closer to the object, only to find that it was a simple wedge – similar to a common doorstop.

Bewildered by how this could be his greatest tool, they turned and looked at the devil inquiringly as if to ask, "What in 'hell' is this?"

"This," the devil smilingly revealed, "is the wedge of self-doubt. With it, I can shatter a person's self-image. I drive this wedge into the back of a person's mind between their abilities and potential. If I create a gap between someone's abilities and what is truly possible for them, I can literally destroy that person. It is worn down so much because I use it with nearly everybody. "

In fact, even a flicker of doubt can paralyze and prevent individuals from achieving their full potential. This, the devil concluded, is what truly hinders most people from leading better lives.

It's true; even the slightest doubt can stop you dead in your tracks. Indeed, it is what hinders most people from leading better lives.

The good news is that doubt is simply a reflection of our self-image. To succeed, you need to change your mindset. Do not allow self-doubt to invade your thoughts. Instead, believe that you have what it takes.

Believing in yourself is a choice. Eliminate the phrase *'I can't'* and all of its cousins, such as *'I wish,' 'I hope,' 'I'm not so sure,' 'It's too hard,'* and so on. These words disempower you – don't use them! Words are powerful. The words you use affect your physiology, which in turn, affects your performance and then your results, and eventually your reality.

James Allen said:

The Magic of Believing

Belief is the basis of all action, and this being so, the belief that dominates the heart or mind is shown in the life.

George Dantzig's story is an exceptional example of the power of belief.

One day in 1939, George Bernard Dantzig, a doctoral candidate at the University of California, Berkeley, arrived late for a graduate-level statistics class and found two problems written on the board. He quickly copied the two math problems on the board, assuming that they were the homework assignments. It took him several days to work through the two problems, but he finally completed them. The next day, he dropped the homework off at the professor's desk.

On a Sunday morning a few days later, George was awakened early by a call from his excited professor. Since George had been late for that class, he hadn't heard the professor announce that the two problems on the board were mathematical mind-teasers that even Einstein hadn't been able to solve. But George Dantzig, believing that he was working on ordinary homework problems, had solved not one but two problems that had stumped mathematicians for hundreds of years!

(Kersey, 1998)

Dantzig's tale is not limited to the field of mathematics. Most restrictions are self-imposed. We set ourselves up for amazing feats when we tackle tasks with a "beginner's mind," devoid of preconceived assumptions of difficulty.

Consider how many great things we could achieve if we just believed that they were possible – or if you *didn't know* you couldn't do it!

How does an individual create this all-important concept called 'belief'?

Through *action!* Action creates belief – burn those words into your memory. It's one of the greatest 'secrets' of success. Here is how it works:

```
┌─────────────────────────────────────┐
│       Action Creates Experience      │
└─────────────────────────────────────┘
                   ▼
┌─────────────────────────────────────┐
│    Experience Creates Competence     │
└─────────────────────────────────────┘
                   ▼
┌─────────────────────────────────────┐
│    Competence Creates Confidence     │
└─────────────────────────────────────┘
                   ▼
┌─────────────────────────────────────┐
│   Confidence Creates Small Successes │
└─────────────────────────────────────┘
                   ▼
┌─────────────────────────────────────┐
│     Small Successes Create Belief    │
└─────────────────────────────────────┘
                   ▼
┌─────────────────────────────────────┐
│      Belief Creates Big Successes    │
└─────────────────────────────────────┘
```

There are numerous books and articles, each presenting a different perspective on manifesting desires. Often, the techniques described require little or no effort. It would be nice if it were that simple, but rarely is it so. Generally, when a person does not take appropriate action (involving the investment of time, effort, money, or resources) to manifest a result, they subconsciously don't feel confident that it will happen.

Imagine you want to win the jackpot in the next lottery or lotto draw, and I ask you, "Did you purchase a lottery ticket?" You give me a glum look and say, "No." Now, you know just as well as I do that because you did not take action, you have absolutely no chance of winning unless someone else buys a ticket for you. You did not act, so you don't believe you can win. The Law of Attraction simply aligns with your belief, and, as a result, you're on the sidelines watching somebody else take the prize.

Merely thinking or talking about success will not create the desired results. When you desire something, but your energy isn't congruent with that desire, it won't come to pass. You have to want something so deeply that your entire being resonates in harmony with that desire – it essentially becomes embedded in your DNA. There can be no discord between what you desire and your vibrational energy. You must walk the talk.

A pivotal moment occurs when belief turns into action. It's that instant when you shift from passive dreaming to active doing. This change is key because it's the catalyst that turns potential into reality. Action is the tangible form of belief, and it's what distinguishes dreamers from achievers.

Expect to Succeed

Living with positive expectancy produces excellent rewards. Have an abundance mentality. Aim high, but be realistic. Setting a goal to fly like a bird without mechanical assistance is unrealistic, given our current understanding of physics.

According to the Law of Expectation, whatever you expect with confidence, positive or negative, *becomes* your reality. If you confidently expect to succeed, you will.

As the following poem describes, you get little if you expect little.

My Wage

I bargained with Life for a penny,
And Life would pay no more,
However I begged at evening
When I counted my scanty store.

For Life is a just employer,
He gives you what you ask,
But once you have set the wages,
Why, you must bear the task.

I worked for a menial's hire,
Only to learn, dismayed,
That any wage I had asked of Life,
Life would have willingly paid.

~ Jessie B. Rittenhouse

William Somerset Maugham said, *"It's a funny thing about life: if you refuse to accept anything but the best, you very often get it."* So, beg boldly because, according to Seneca, *"he who begs timidly courts a refusal."* Our problem is that we ask too little from life, mainly due to our conditioning or programming.

Social Programming

What happens to the dreams we had as kids? Unfortunately, they often get lost along the way. This is because we're influenced by the people and things around us without realizing it. This influence is called social or enculturation programming.

Enculturation programming is like a silent teacher that shapes our beliefs and behaviors without us noticing. It happens through daily interactions with others, like parents, siblings, teachers, coworkers, and the media. These interactions tell us what life is about and how we should live it.

A study at the University of Iowa found that the average two-year-old hears 432 negative comments daily, but only 32 positive ones. This 14-to-1 ratio shows just how much negative feedback we're exposed to in our early years.

As we grow up, we're taught to fit in with what's considered "normal" – to stay within the lines, keep our dreams in check, and let go of our make-believe companions and spirits. We learn that specific actions get attention, and we're praised or reprimanded accordingly. This shapes our behavior over time. Once these behaviors are ingrained, they become a part of our consciousness and are difficult to change.

Some of the programming we receive is obvious, but much of it is subtle. Every day, we're bombarded with instructions, advice, directions, and expectations. This can have a significant impact on us, whether we're aware of it or not.

Not all of our programming is bad, of course. Some of it helps us be happy, healthy, and safe. But a lot of it can hold us back, stifling our creativity and making us miss out on opportunities. As a result, we develop our core beliefs, which shape our distinctive personalities and individual realities. These beliefs are our perceptions of how life works, but they're not always true.

Some beliefs literally put a lid on our potential. Experiments show humans and animals react similarly to reinforcement. Here are two examples:

Fleas in a Jar

Fleas are astonishing jumpers, capable of leaping over 150 times their own height. In an experiment, a scientist placed several fleas in a glass jar. As expected, they quickly jumped out. The scientist then returned the fleas to the jar and covered it with a glass lid. Initially, the fleas jumped freely, hitting the lid and falling back down. After a while, however, they adapted their behavior. Conditioned by the presence of the lid, they began jumping to a lower height to avoid hitting it.

One might argue the fleas were being clever, learning to avoid a futile endeavor.

However, the true test came when the scientist removed the lid entirely. The fleas continued jumping at their self-imposed "safe" height despite the newfound freedom. They had become accustomed to the limitation and, in a sense, internalized it. The jar remained their prison, not because of the physical barrier but because of their conditioned behavior.

The Pike Experiment

A pike fish was put in a tank with many small minnows. The pike wasted no time eating all the minnows.

The next day, a glass partition was placed into the tank, dividing the tank into two. At feeding time, instead of putting the live minnows in with the pike, the minnows were placed on the other side of the partition. The pike could see the minnows but could not get to them. Unable to detect the glass divider, the pike repeatedly slammed its head against it in pursuit of its meal. After countless failed attempts, it gave up entirely.

Days later, the glass partition was removed from the tank allowing the pike to swim freely amongst the minnows. It could now easily eat the minnows, but the strangest thing happened. Even though the pike hadn't eaten in days and the minnows were within easy reach, it made no attempt to hunt. The relentless frustration of its prior attempts had sapped its will to hunt. Surrounded by food, the pike perished.

Like other creatures, humans naturally tend to adapt to our environment and learn from our experiences. If we keep failing, eventually, we just stop trying. Science and industry are full of examples showing how limiting beliefs impede progress until someone breaks through, and suddenly, a host of others follow. Two fascinating stories demonstrate this:

The Vasily Alexeev Story

Vasily Alexeev, a Soviet weightlifting legend, was the first to conquer the seemingly insurmountable barrier of lifting 500 pounds. However, his journey to this record-breaking feat was not without its challenges. Alexeev initially plateaued at 499 pounds, convinced it was his absolute limit.

His trainers, determined to shatter this mental barrier, devised a clever ploy. They rigged the barbell to appear as if it held 499 pounds, while secretly loading it with 501.5 pounds. Unaware of the deception, Alexeev lifted the weight with surprising ease.

This seemingly small deception shattered a mental barrier, proving to Alexeev (and the weightlifting world) that 500 pounds was not an impossible feat. Soon after that, other weightlifters went on to break his record because they now knew it was possible to lift more than 500 pounds.

The Roger Bannister Story

For decades, the four-minute mile was considered an insurmountable barrier in athletics. Scientists believed the human body simply couldn't withstand the physical demands of running a mile at such a blistering pace. Then came Roger Bannister. In 1954, he defied these limitations, shattering the record and clocking in at an astonishing 3:59.4.

This feat proved to be a watershed moment. Within a year, 37 other runners broke the four-minute barrier, followed by another 300 within three years. Today, thousands have surpassed this once-unthinkable feat, constantly pushing the boundaries of human potential.

The mile run is no longer an Olympic or World Championship event, but its legacy endures. The current world record of 3:43.13, set by Hicham El Guerrouj in 1999, is proof of the transformative power of breaking down perceived limitations.

These examples show that the only limitations we have are those we place on ourselves. After a few unsuccessful attempts (similar to the fleas and pike fish), we tend to avoid actions associated with pain or failure. While avoiding destructive behaviors makes sense, we also tend to shy away from challenges that could lead to growth. We often say, "Been there; done that; it doesn't work," and move on to easier options.

Instead of accepting easy options, we must embrace the challenging journey of life and recognize that our social environment has unconsciously shaped our preferences, beliefs, and attitudes.

To change our outcomes, we must change our programming by questioning our beliefs. Our beliefs influence our choices and opportunities. In the end, our success or failure is based on what we believe is possible. By overcoming our self-imposed limitations, we can gain new insights and achieve our goals.

Genes and Success

Some believe that genes and the environment work together to determine an individual's propensity for success in life. While it is clear that the environment in which we operate definitely influences our propensity for success, there is no clear evidence to show that our genes play any role whatsoever. Nevertheless, it is important to recognize that our genes are an integral part of who we are, but we have the power to shape our experiences and outcomes through our beliefs, choices, and actions.

In fact, it is said that our beliefs control our genes (or genetic makeup), and not our genes control our beliefs. It is our beliefs, and how we understand life, that determines which genes will be activated to determine the nature of our continued existence. So, in all likelihood, genes have little direct influence on your results in life. You are not a victim of your genes, which you received at birth from your parents. So, don't blame your genes (or your parents) for your circumstances. If you are in any way a victim, then you might be a victim of memes (which rhymes with genes).

Going Beyond Your Genes... to Memes!

Genes are said to transmit biological information, and memes transmit ideas and belief information. "A meme is 'an idea, behavior or style' that spreads through a sociological culture, from one person to another, similar to the behavior of a virus." (Meme, 2012)

Memes are cultural elements that significantly influence our thoughts and actions. They can influence an entire sociological culture and explain why certain groups hold particular beliefs. By examining memes, we can gain insight into the values and beliefs of a group and understand how culture shapes our beliefs and actions.

Here is a classic example of how a meme spreads by itself.

The Hundredth Monkey Phenomenon

The Japanese monkey, Macaca fuscata, had been observed in the wild for a period of over thirty years.

In 1952, on the island of Koshima, scientists were providing monkeys with sweet potatoes dropped in the sand. The monkeys liked the taste of the raw sweet potatoes, but they found the dirt unpleasant. An 18-month-old female (named Imo) found she could get rid of the sand by washing the potatoes in a nearby stream. She taught this trick to her mother and her playmates; they taught their mothers, too.

This cultural innovation was gradually picked up, and between 1952 and 1958, all the young monkeys learned to wash the sandy sweet potatoes to make them more palatable. Only the adults who imitated their children learned this social improvement. Other adults kept eating the dirty sweet potatoes.

One day in 1958, something interesting happened. A certain number of Koshima monkeys were washing sweet potatoes. The exact number is not known. Let's assume that there were 99 monkeys washing potatoes. Let's further assume that later that morning, the hundredth monkey learned to wash potatoes.

Then a most amazing phenomenon occurred!

By that evening, almost every monkey in the tribe was washing sweet potatoes before eating them. The added energy of this hundredth monkey somehow created an ideological breakthrough!

But it didn't end there. A most surprising thing observed by these scientists was that the monkeys' habit of washing sweet potatoes then jumped across the sea.

Colonies of monkeys on other islands and the mainland troop of monkeys at Takasakiyama began washing their sweet potatoes too!

Thus, when a certain critical number achieves an awareness, this new awareness may be communicated from mind to mind. Although the exact number may vary, this Hundredth Monkey Phenomenon means that when only a limited number of people know of a new way, it may remain the conscious property of these people. But there is a point at which, if only one more person tunes in to a new awareness, an energy field is strengthened so that this awareness is picked up by almost everyone!

(The Hundredth Monkey Phenomenon, 2009)

The story explains how information can spread subliminally across physical boundaries, influencing individuals and groups without their awareness. This phenomenon highlights the power of energy and the interconnectedness of all things.

When a meme (an idea or behavior) becomes established in science or academia, it becomes a paradigm – a set of beliefs, assumptions, and values that influence how we perceive and interpret reality. Our subconscious mind acts as a storehouse of information, absorbing everything we feed it, regardless of its truth or accuracy. Whether outdated, negative, or incorrect, this information influences our daily decisions.

Adopting a paradigm, consciously or subconsciously, shapes our belief system and life. Negative paradigms, such as "life is a struggle" or "I'm a victim," can hinder progress. Conversely, positive paradigms, like "I succeed" or "I'm responsible for my outcomes," can push us forward.

Our destiny isn't fixed. Past patterns don't dictate future outcomes. Allowing negative paradigms to persist empowers our past over our present.

The first step in shifting paradigms is to acknowledge the problem: we have been subliminally programmed by our environment and have developed limiting beliefs. By recognizing this, we can consciously shift our thinking and create new, empowering beliefs.

You Can't Fix a Problem That You Don't Acknowledge

The Alcoholics Anonymous (AA) program is based on twelve steps. When someone joins AA, the first step is to admit powerlessness over alcohol and an unmanageable life. Recovery is impossible without recognizing the reality of the problem.

According to AA, the first step toward change is admitting the need for change. In essence, you can't fix a problem you don't acknowledge.

Bestselling author Stephen R. Covey said:

> *Until a person can say deeply and honestly, 'I am what I am today because of the choices I made yesterday,' that person cannot say, 'I choose otherwise'.*

In the same way, you must acknowledge that you have unwittingly developed some limiting beliefs through social programming. You cannot succeed with negative beliefs. A paradigm shift is essential.

Moving forward, take a moment to consider the profound power of belief and its impact on your life. Challenge yourself to question your long-held beliefs. Are they serving you, or are they holding you back? Be willing to let go of the beliefs that no longer serve you and embrace new, empowering paradigms that support your goals and aspirations.

Remember, the magic of believing is not just a concept – it's a powerful tool that you now possess. Use it wisely and often, and watch as it transforms your life in ways you never thought possible.

In the following chapters, we'll examine practical strategies to reshape your beliefs, harness the power of positive expectations, and create a mindset that attracts success. Your journey to success continues with the simple yet powerful act of believing in your dreams and your ability to realize them.

Hidden truths:

1. Believing is seeing; not seeing is believing.
2. Action creates belief.
3. Your subconscious mind will accept whatever you feed it, whether it is true or not.
4. Social programming is transmitted across physical boundaries; it can be adopted without us even being aware of it.
5. Until you acknowledge your limiting beliefs you cannot begin the process of effective change – you can't fix a problem that you don't acknowledge.

Chapter 8

The Fast Track to Creating What You Want

The Law of Manifestation is central to the Law of Attraction. It explains how our thoughts, beliefs, and emotions can shape our reality, allowing us to create the life we envision.

The key to releasing its power lies in five key steps:

1. **Ignite a Burning Desire**
   Develop a deep and passionate desire for success. This desire must be fueled by a strong belief in your ability to achieve it.

2. **Define Your Goal with Clarity**
   Express your goal in precise, positive terms. "Name it to claim it" – the more specific you are, the more effective the manifestation.

3. **Visualize with Emotion**
   Vividly imagine your goal as already achieved. The more emotionally charged your visualization, the stronger the magnetism drawing your desire towards you.

4. **Embrace Divine Guidance**
   Be receptive to the signs and synchronicities the universe provides. Trust that you are supported on your journey, even when the path isn't clear.

5. **Act on Your Intuition**
   Follow your intuition; it's your compass guiding you to the right actions and opportunities, even when logic doesn't make sense.

Let's break down each of these impactful steps in more detail:

8.1 Ignite a Burning Desire

A *burning* desire is the first ingredient of success. To simply desire is one thing; to burn with conviction is another thing entirely. Every success story begins with a burning desire. The intensity of your desire significantly influences your success in any endeavor.

Your desire to achieve must be so strong that it keeps you awake at night and dominates your thoughts. If you don't feel that level of urgency, your desire is merely lukewarm – not really a burning desire.

A burning desire is intense and urgent instead of something nice to have, like desiring an ice cream. It is to success what rocket fuel is to a rocket engine. It propels you into action. A burning desire is a creative power that *has* to manifest or express itself in the external world. It is an emotional force that attracts. The emotion attached to your desire moves you towards your desired outcome and magnetically draws your desired outcome towards you. A burning desire has a sense of desperation, and as an ingredient of success, it is comparable to air, the most basic element for life's sustenance. The following story illustrates:

A Student's Quest for Success

A student, eager for a shortcut to success, approached his spiritual teacher for guidance. The teacher smiled knowingly and instructed, "Meet me at the Ganges River at 5:00 am tomorrow." Intrigued, the student arrived on time, finding his teacher wading in the river, beckoning him to join. Wanting to uncover the secret to success, the student complied.

Suddenly, the teacher submerged the student's head underwater. Gasping for air, the student struggled, panicking. The teacher held him down for what felt like an eternity before finally releasing him.

Sputtering, the student demanded, "Why did you do that?" The calm teacher responded, "While you were underwater, what consumed your thoughts? Success? Wealth? Recognition?"

The student, catching his breath, replied, "No, sir. All I craved was air. Nothing but air."

The teacher's message was clear: "If you desire success with the same relentless intensity that you desired that breath of air, success will be yours. It will come to you as swiftly as you desire."

This story illustrates that true success requires an all-consuming drive – an intensity that mirrors the desperate need for air. Consider your daily actions: do they reflect a burning desire for your goals, or are they half-hearted attempts? An unshakeable hunger for success is necessary to endure the relentless effort required to achieve it.

Particularly, your goals must be personal; they should stem from your deep desires rather than from others' expectations. It is said, "The hand will not reach for what the heart does not long for." Your desires should stir a feeling that motivates you to take action each morning. If they don't, you'll likely give up when faced with challenges.

To be considered a burning desire, your goal must rank at 100 on a scale of 1 to 100. Anything less, even a 99, is insufficient.

Consider this analogy: If you heat water to 99°C, you can make a great cup of tea. But, at 100°C, it boils and generates steam – powerful enough to move a steamship or a locomotive. That one degree makes a monumental difference.

To achieve your goal, you must be "steaming" with emotion to:

- Learn whatever you need to learn
- Become whatever you need to become
- Do whatever you need to do
- Have whatever you want to have

You can tell how badly you want to achieve your goal by observing your daily actions. When you possess a burning desire, you'll do whatever it takes to make it happen. If you don't have a "Damn the torpedoes, full speed ahead!" attitude, it indicates you haven't reached 100 on the scale.

Achieving your goal is not about ability or intellect; it's about heartfelt desire. Genuine desire focuses your attention, establishes commitment, and empowers you to tackle any challenge. As you are driven forward by your desire, you'll hardly notice the effort. You'll develop new skills, beliefs, attitudes, and a new sense of self – an entirely new consciousness!

An Enlightened Thought for Reflection

You are what your deep driving desire is;
As your deep driving desire is, so is your will;
As your will is, so is your deed;
As your deed is, so is your destiny.

~ Maitri Upanishads

8.2   Define Your Goal with Clarity

Imagine being blindfolded, holding a dart, and told to hit a target on a wall. Unless you have extrasensory perception, you wouldn't know where to aim. Similarly, achieving a goal you haven't clearly defined is incredibly challenging.

Your Magnificent Vision

Every worthwhile accomplishment begins with a vision. Vision is the art of seeing the invisible – seeing something with your *mind* before seeing it with your eyes. You can accomplish the impossible if you can see the invisible.

You can truly have whatever you want, regardless of how absurd it may appear initially. For change to occur, you must replace your old vision with a new one. Steve Jobs, co-founder of Apple Inc., envisioned creating groundbreaking products for everyday people. His vision led to Apple becoming synonymous with innovation. Remarkably, Jobs conceptualized the iPad 30 years before its success!

The wealthiest and most successful individuals have a magnificent vision of the lives they wish to lead. They create clear mental images of what they want in critical areas: health, wealth, relationships, spirituality, and more. They articulate their dreams into specific goals for each area of life and then develop plans to achieve them.

Clearly Define Your Goal

Mark Twain said, *"I can teach anybody to get whatever they want out of life. The problem is that I can't find anybody who can tell me what they want."*

Whatever you desire must first be clearly defined. You must stake your claim to your desired outcome – draw a line in the sand. The most you'll ever get from life is what you ask for. Simply thinking about what you want is a good start, but you need to write a goal statement. Specify exactly what you want and the date by which you intend to achieve it.

Most people fail to reach their goals because they lack awareness of the goal-setting process. This leads to a division between "winners" and "losers." Winners often have written goals and detailed plans to achieve them. They know where they are going and how to get there. It is for good reason a bank won't lend money to a business owner without a written business plan.

Scott Adams, creator of "Dilbert," is one of the most successful cartoonists in history. A firm believer in written goals and affirmations, he wrote, "I, Scott Adams, am a successful syndicated cartoonist," 15 times every day for six months. When faced with doubts, he thought, "What do I have to lose?" After many rejections and through perseverance, Scott achieved his goal of becoming a syndicated cartoonist in over 2,000 newspapers worldwide.

Writing down your goals clarifies your thinking and generates goal-oriented thoughts. Once you define what you want to achieve, it becomes easier to manifest – 'a problem defined is a problem half-solved.' In medicine, a correct diagnosis is half the cure. Similarly, a written goal is a significant step towards fulfillment.

Written goals possess incredible power. They provide direction in your life and empower you to face the future with determination. By committing your goals to paper, you infuse them with energy, significantly increasing the likelihood of their manifestation.

Here are several reasons why writing down your goals is so impactful:

1. Writing down your goals forces you to define what you want. There's truth in the saying, "You have to name it to claim it."

2. Written goals allow you to be specific about what you want. Most people underestimate the importance of specificity. A clear goal leads to clearer results.

3. There is energy in the written word. Everything is energy, including your written words, which emit vibrations that attract accordingly.

4. Written goals help you focus on turning your dreams into reality.

When writing down your goals, apply the SMART criteria. Although the meanings of the letters can vary (for example, 'R' can mean 'Realistic' or 'T' can mean 'Timely'), the commonly accepted values are:

- **Specific:** The goal must clearly describe the desired outcome.
- **Measurable:** The goal's performance must be measurable.
- **Attainable:** The goal should be challenging yet achievable.
- **Relevant:** The goal must be something you genuinely want.
- **Time-bound:** The goal must have a specific time frame or deadline.

Write your goal in the present tense as if you have already achieved it. For instance, if your goal is to lose a specific amount of weight by a certain date, you might write:

"It is September 30, 2029. I now weigh 62 kilos. I enjoy my healthy eating plan and feel exhilarated when I exercise. I love my body and treat it with respect. I feel proud of my healthy lifestyle and am thrilled with all the compliments I receive."

Your SMART goal becomes your target destination. While studies show that writing down your goal increases your chances of achieving it, developing a detailed action plan is equally essential to reaching your destination.

8.3 Visualize with Emotion

To manifest your dreams, you must first visualize them in your mind. What you "see" will come to be! What you continually picture in your mind will eventually manifest in reality. Your subconscious mind obeys the images you create in your imagination.

An Enlightened Thought for Reflection

Your imagination is your preview of life's coming attractions.

~ *Albert Einstein*

So, how does visualization really work?

Visualization uses your imagination to channel creative energies toward your desired outcome. Whatever you focus your attention on will grow stronger in your life. Whatever you take your attention away from will grow weaker and cease to exist over time. Why is this so? Because where attention goes, energy flows. The process of manifestation is attention. To expedite achieving your goals, consistently visualize them and get emotional about them – see them as already accomplished.

We inherently think in pictures (or images). If I say "hamburger," you immediately envision one. If I mention "pink elephant" or "yellow sports car," those images come to mind. Therefore, having a clear mental picture of your desired outcome aligns with how our minds naturally function.

The image you hold in your mind, positive or negative, will seek expression in the physical world. Your subconscious will take the image of your desire and turn it into vibrations that attract the ideas, resources, and circumstances necessary to bring it to fruition.

Try this exercise:

Activating the Law of Attraction is like turning on a switch. Create a vision board filled with images of all you desire: a new house, a new car, a better career, a healthier body, a new relationship, and more. This process will help clarify what you truly want.

Choose images that evoke an emotional response. Looking at the picture should inspire joy and excitement; this emotional connection is imperative. Place your vision board where you'll see it daily. Each time you look at it, envision yourself in those images. Feel what it's like to already possess and experience what they represent.

The stronger your vibrational energy, the faster you attract the resources and situations necessary to manifest your desires. Also, recognize that if you cannot envision a way out of an unfavorable situation, you'll remain stuck indefinitely. Always visualize what you want, not what you don't want!

In addition to a vision board, consider other ways to accelerate your manifestation process:

1. Place a picture of what you desire, such as a million-dollar check, on your ceiling so you can view it before sleeping and upon waking up.
2. Display images at your workplace, on your fridge, or on your bathroom mirror.
3. Create a custom screensaver for your computer or phone.

Jim Carrey is a prime example of how powerful focused intent can be:

> Jim Carrey's journey to Hollywood stardom substantiates the power of focused ambition. Long before his name became synonymous with comedic brilliance, Carrey harbored a burning desire for wealth and fame. According to Biography Channel, he manifested this dream in a unique way: by writing himself a post-dated check for $10 million, payable on Thanksgiving 1995. The memo line read, "For Acting Services Rendered." At the time, Carrey's bank account barely held ten thousand dollars, starkly contrasting the amount he envisioned.

Undeterred by this financial gap, Carrey maintained a steadfast faith in his aspirations. The road to success, though, was paved with challenges. He encountered obstacles that might have discouraged lesser spirits, but Carrey persevered. His relentless drive propelled him forward, and his gamble on his own potential paid off in spectacular fashion.

Carrey's career skyrocketed, surpassing the $10 million mark many times over. He commanded a staggering $20 million salary for "The Cable Guy" in 1996, followed by another $20 million for "Liar Liar" in 1997. By 2003, his fee for "Bruce Almighty" had climbed to $25 million. Reports suggest his average earnings per film has since exceeded $20 million! (wiki.answers.com)

Carrey's experience is not unusual; many high achievers have similar stories.

The following is an inspiring story told by motivational speaker Skip Ross that effectively illustrates the process of manifestation using imagery and living the experience.

The Maserati

A businessman dreamt of owning a Maserati as a reward for achieving a specific income goal. He cut out a full-page picture of his desired car from a "Wheels" magazine and proudly displayed it on his wall.

He drove a worn-out old car at the time, but his imagination transformed him into a Maserati owner whenever he was behind the wheel. He'd carefully back out of the garage, imagining his neighbors watching as he cruised off with the windows down, reveling in the luxury of leather seats, a wood-grain dashboard, and a premium sound system. Even at traffic lights, he envisioned other drivers admiring his imaginary Maserati.

Years later, he finally reached his financial target and walked into a dealership, excited to choose the exact color of his dream car.

A few weeks later, the dealership contacted him for a special "presentation" to receive it. However, upon arrival, he encountered a problem: "This isn't the exact color I ordered," he pointed out, noting the slight shade difference.

The dealership acknowledged the error and offered a significant discount, but the customer remained dissatisfied. He refused their offer, expressing disappointment over the color. The officials huddled together and returned with another proposal: they had a Maserati in his desired color, but it was a more expensive sports edition and formerly a show car featuring thousands of dollars in extras. Despite being a more expensive edition, they offered it at no extra cost.

Hesitant, he replied, "I didn't wait all this time for a used car." The officials insisted, "It's not a used car; it's practically new with minimal mileage." They encouraged him to at least see the car before making a final decision. Initially resistant, he agreed to check it only to confirm the color.

Upon entering the showroom, he was speechless. The car exceeded even his wildest dreams. Concealing his excitement from the salespeople, he meticulously inspected the vehicle for flaws, finding none. Thrilled by its upgraded features, he finally said, "Alright, I'll take it." Everyone involved was pleased.

After the presentation, he proudly drove his dream car home. As he entered his house, he glanced at the Maserati picture on his wall and suddenly realized that the car parked in his driveway was the exact one in the picture! It was a snapshot of his very own Maserati from a motor show – a testament to the power of visualization and steadfast determination.

This is not a coincidence but rather the precise operation of the Law of Attraction. If you put in your best effort, the Universe will unfailingly deliver!

8.4   Embrace Divine Guidance

The universe is a living, breathing entity. All its life forms – human, animal, plant, mineral, fungi, and bacteria – are interconnected and correspond with each other in some way. To accelerate the manifestation process, you must remain open-minded and aware of this connectedness.

The universe knows your desires but only grants you what you're ready for. Your intense desire will create a flow of synchronous events, both positive and negative, to manifest your outcome. Be mindful of the possibilities that arise along your path.

Synchronicity

Synchronicity happens regardless of whether you are aware of it. It's often described as the opposite of coincidence – while coincidences are random and meaningless, synchronicities appear divinely orchestrated, arriving precisely when needed.

According to Wikipedia, synchronicity is the experience of two or more causally unrelated events occurring together meaningfully. For an event to qualify as synchronicity, it should be unlikely to happen together by chance.

Typical examples include:

- Alexander Fleming's discovery of penicillin occurred when he "failed" to disinfect bacteria cultures, which became contaminated with penicillium molds that killed the bacteria.
- While visiting a bookstore, uncertain of what to buy, the exact book you need falls off the shelf and nearly hits you.
- In a rush, you arrive at a place where parking is scarce, and someone pulls out of a spot just as you arrive.
- You're focused on finding your soulmate, and shortly after, your cab driver drops you off at the wrong terminal, leading you to meet the love of your life, who missed their flight.

Nothing in your life is coincidental. Events happen for a reason, even if they seem uncanny. Consider the following story:

Snapshot at Lourdes

Carol Anderson was a young widow whose husband had died of cancer at thirty-five. Bob Edwards was a young widower whose wife had been killed in a car accident at twenty-nine. Both marriages had been extremely happy, and both Carol and Bob were sure they would never love or marry again. After many lonely years of pain and suffering, they met at a church dinner and started courting. When they got engaged and then married, they told everyone that it was miraculous that they had found each other. Their relationship was strong and loving. The only trouble spot in the marriage was that they had diametrically different opinions on what to do about the past.

Carol longed to bury it; Bob needed to explore it. Carol never wanted to talk about either of their previous marriages. Bob, on the other hand, was eager to know the most minute details of Carol's life before they had met and was hurt that Carol showed such a complete lack of interest in his.

"Why raise ghosts?" Carol would ask when Bob would persist with his gentle probing and soft inquiries.

"Memory should be preserved, not obliterated," he would reply. This went on for years, with Carol's perspective ultimately prevailing. As a result, they never shared stories, pictures, or mementos from their first marriages.

Ten years later, Carol felt their marriage was secure enough to withstand any assaults from the past. "Okay," she told Bob one day, "I'm ready to talk." She began telling Bob about her first marriage and pulled out several snapshots and albums she had hidden from him all these years. "These are from our honeymoon," she said, starting to leaf through the pages of one album. "We went to France. Oh, here we are at Lourdes."

"You went to Lourdes?" Bob said with mild interest. "So did we."

"Well, I guess half the world goes to Lourdes," Carol laughed. "No big deal. Everyone was looking for blessings and miracles in their lives."

"Wait a second, Carol, turn back a page," said Bob suddenly. "Let me see the snapshot again of you and Ralph at Lourdes."

Carol obligingly turned back a page.

"Carol," her husband asked tensely, "who is that couple in the background?"

"I have no idea, *she said*. Just as the photographer snapped the picture, a couple walked by and got caught by the shutter. I can see why you asked, though, thinking they were with us. In the picture, it does look as though they're standing behind us, almost as if they're posing, but it's just an illusion."

"You're wrong, Carol," Bob said slowly. "It wasn't a mistake; it was destiny. You see, that couple in the background was me and my first wife."

Comment:

Millions of people travel to Lourdes each year. What were the chances of Carol and Bob being at the same place at the same time and coincidentally appearing together in a photo at the holy shrine? When the picture was taken, they lived in different parts of the United States and were not members of the same association, organization, or tour group. They were not connected in any way – except in God's plan. The people who make pilgrimages to Lourdes are, more often than not, the ill, the infirm, and the elderly, rather than young people like Carol and Bob. Life had just begun for each couple, and seemingly neither Bob nor Carol needed a miracle. But they did get a miracle… only they hadn't known it then.

(Halberstam, Y., & Leventhal, J. 1997)

When events like this happen, it can certainly make you wonder about the concepts of destiny and free will. Are events like these predestined or unconsciously shaped by earlier thoughts, words, deeds, or feelings that led to such an outcome?

There are *always* countless synchronous events occurring around you, many of which can be life-changing. Only when you open your mind to the possibility of synchronicity and the fact that these events happen all the time around you will you recognize them as being *divinely orchestrated*.

The Universe is constantly orchestrating your life's journey and creating meaningful coincidences for you. If you are not open to the possibility of synchronicity, then you will not recognize synchronous events when they occur. They could be as subtle as a hunch that you should join your local library, even though you hadn't planned to – and then you meet the love of your life there.

Synchronicity is a sign that the Law of Attraction is at work. Synchronous events tend to occur more frequently when you are deeply caught up or focused on something. When you have a constant burning desire, you subconsciously send a message to the Universe requesting a specific outcome. So, the Universe goes to work, lining up the people, resources, and situations needed to manifest that outcome. Ideas, feelings, chance meetings, valuable encounters, and timely opportunities, all seemingly coincidental, will present themselves to you.

Pay attention to these coincidental events and see if they connect meaningfully to your desired outcome. The connectivity is a sign that the Universe is processing your request. When you recognize it, your confidence will grow astronomically!

The more open and aware you are, the more you will experience synchronous events in your life. To increase your chances of synchronicity, go out into the world and experience life. Don't stay trapped inside your house waiting for something to drop into your lap while watching TV.

Get out of the house! Meet new people. Join clubs, visit libraries, and socialize with like-minded individuals to exchange ideas on mutual interests.

Be open to guidance and embrace what develops; synchronous events will unfold naturally and effortlessly. Participate in the unfolding events, and the Universe will guide you toward your desired outcome.

8.5   Act on Your Intuition

The path to success is not accidental; it's a planned journey. Successful people don't start out successful. They begin with a dream and a burning desire to make that dream a reality. Then, they plan their work and diligently work that plan.

You cannot bring your desires to fruition without taking effective action. Without action, your vision remains an unfulfilled dream. Success involves deciding what you want and taking step-by-step actions to achieve it.

Remember, you are a magnet that attracts. Most often, you won't attract what you want directly. Instead, opportunities presented by the universe will come as intuitive prompts nudging you to act or go somewhere.

These prompts may manifest as emotions, gut feelings, inner voices, or nudges to take a specific action. Whatever form it takes, trust your intuition and act on it. You'll find that synchronicities occur more frequently.

Intuition is often described as immediate knowing – sensing the truth without explanations and the conscious use of the intellect. It transcends the intellect and is about following your heart rather than your head.

We all possess intuition, an innate ability to know something without explanation. For example, you might sense when someone is looking at you from across the room or feel when something is amiss. We are all born with it, and it serves our well-being. Some people have stronger intuitive powers than others, either inherited or gained through practice.

If it feels right, follow your intuition. You never know where it might lead. When you are attuned to receiving the seeds of opportunity, even if it is based on a *gut feeling*, the Universe will guide you to the right place at the right time, as it did for Shelley in the following story.

Shelley received a much-needed gift in a very unusual way. She was sitting at Notre Dame in Paris, resting her sore feet. She had not carried comfortable shoes from home in the States, and her limited budget wouldn't allow her to buy another pair although her feet ached terribly.

Suddenly, she felt the urge to leave the church and turn left. Following her instincts, she made several more turns until she arrived at a square. To her surprise, she spotted a pair of brand-new black boots, exactly her size, on top of a trash can. She realized the situation was perfect and had been arranged specifically for her. If the boots had been in the trash can, she wouldn't have taken them. If they had been worn before, she wouldn't have put them on. They were also so stylish that she could not have afforded them herself!

Would this be a story of intuition or synchronicity? Intuition appeared to have led her to the boots. Synchronicity provided her with precisely what she needed. The Universe virtually handed her the boots.

(Lundstrom, M., 1996)

You can improve your intuitive ability, just as with any new skill. The more you practice, the better you become. Courage is essential; it requires listening to your inner guide and acting on the received guidance. Intuitive knowing works best in the moment.

Listening to your intuition connects you with your higher self – the divine within. It can be a valuable guide as you take the step-by-step actions necessary to achieve your desired outcome in life.

Your path to success is not accidental; it's a journey you design. As you move forward, understand the following fundamental principles:

1. A *burning desire* is not just a want but a passionate drive that thrusts you into action.
2. When combined with *clear, specific goals*, you increase your chances of success and create a more fulfilling journey.
3. Your ability to *visualize and feel* your desired outcome as if it's already achieved is a fundamental step in the manifestation process.
4. Stay open to *divine guidance and synchronicity* as the universe constantly sends you messages and opportunities. Be receptive and act on them.
5. Trust your *intuition*, as it's your direct line to universal wisdom.

By integrating these five key steps, you release your extraordinary potential and manifest the life of your dreams.

Your journey of conscious creation continues.

Hidden Truths:

1. A burning desire is the first ingredient of success.
2. Whatever you want must be personal; it must be something that you really want for yourself.

3. To speed up the process of manifesting what you want, make a list of the things you desire most. Committing your goals to paper infuses them with energy.

4. The universe knows what you want, but will only give you what you deserve.

5. Intuition transcends the intellect; it connects you with your higher self – the God within.

PART 3

The Law of Action

Chapter 9

Just Be a Better You!

An Enlightened Thought for Reflection

Every man [or woman] is where he is by the Law of his Being.

~ *James Allen*

The Law of Being is fundamental to the Law of Action. Numerous actions can lead you toward your desired outcome. Many of these are task-oriented, but they must be transcended by creating a better version of yourself. Remember the profound words of James Allen: *"People do not attract that which they want, but that which they* are." The Law of Action encompasses both *being* and *doing*. For example, if you wish to attract a new partner into your life, you must radiate love and create space for that special someone.

Wolfgang von Goethe said:

Before you can do something, you must first be something.

According to the Law of Being, your circumstances directly reflect your inner state of being – your vibrational frequency. To change your outer world, you must change your inner vibration.

Your life improves when you improve. There is virtually no limit to how much better you can become by developing your character. Transforming who you are transforms your life circumstances. When your inner state aligns with your desires, you can have whatever you commit to becoming.

Developing a wide range of character virtues is the foundation for true success. Good character comes from practicing virtues, which change your inner state of being. If you strive for a virtuous life, you will experience greater happiness and self-fulfillment and accomplish your highest goals. You will also benefit those around you and contribute positively to society. Without inner change, your being remains the same, producing the same results.

Bestselling author John Kalench posed a compelling question: What is most important in life – to BE, to DO, or to HAVE?

Here's his perspective:

> *You must be absolutely clear on what type of person you want to BE. When you decide this, you can easily choose what you DO to express the person you want to BE. In the process of doing things that are in alignment with who you want to BE, you can't help but unleash passion in what you DO. The result is that you end up loving passionately what you DO, which makes you so much more productive. And in the process of being more productive, you get everything in life you want to HAVE. Therefore, life is not about HAVING to DO to BE – instead, life is about BEING and DOING to HAVE!*
>
> ~ John Kalench

Now, let's consider essential character virtues you need to 'BE' in order to create the outcomes you desire.

116

9.1   Be Prepared…and Opportunity Will Find You

An Enlightened Thought for Reflection

Luck is what happens when preparation meets opportunity.

~ Seneca

Overnight success is a myth. You've likely heard the saying, "It took me 20 years to become an overnight success!" Opportunities rarely just fall into your lap. You must prepare to attract them through research, planning, learning, and taking corrective actions.

As Ben Franklin wisely noted: *"Failing to prepare is preparing to fail."* Most people fail to prepare for the opportunities that are constantly staring them in the face – this prevents them from capitalizing on them. In the game of life, many choose to play it safe, which is playing 'not to lose.' This is a defensive, fear-based approach and a miserable way to live. With such a strategy, you eventually lose anyway. To win at life, it's important to have an offensive strategy and proactively shape events.

An opportunity arises only when you prepare for it by improving yourself and taking goal-directed actions that signal to the Universe your sincere expectation for manifestation. When you genuinely prepare, the Universe will present you with opportunities, and you will recognize them, even when they appear disguised. You may be amazed at how closely these opportunities correspond with your distinct skills and abilities, which you have worked hard to develop!

We live in an information age, a time of profound transformation, especially with the advent of artificial intelligence (AI). Today, success isn't just about having knowledge but knowing how to use it wisely. Knowledge is the fuel that drives progress. It's the secret ingredient to creating value and making a difference. The information revolution empowers those who can harness its power.

Ongoing learning is essential for advancement in any field. The more you learn, the more you earn. The more you know, the better you become at solving problems and achieving results that others will pay for. Knowledge opens doors to freedom and opportunity. The faster and the more you learn, the quicker you advance in your career and all areas of life.

Consider Nelson Mandela, the former President of South Africa, who spent 27 years in prison preparing himself to lead a nation in distress. He used that time to educate and equip himself for a brighter future, eventually guiding his people to freedom. Like Mandela, everyone who has achieved notable success has meticulously prepared for their opportunities.

Continuous improvement may sound cliché, but those who accumulate and apply knowledge across all aspects of their field will rise to the top. It's important to benchmark your progress against others, not just yourself. If you're improving, but others are progressing faster, you are still falling behind! The pursuit of continuous improvement builds character and nurtures a better version of yourself.

Winston Churchill said:

> To every man [or woman], there comes in his lifetime that special moment when he is figuratively tapped on the shoulder and offered a chance to do a very special thing, unique to him and fitted to his talents; what a tragedy if that moment finds him unprepared or unqualified for that which would be his finest hour.

Truly successful individuals are committed to lifelong learning, continually developing themselves, and preparing for even greater opportunities. This journey is not a burden; it is an exciting journey of exploration and personal growth. Success requires you never to stop preparing for the day your opportunity presents itself.

9.2 Be Optimistic – It Makes All The Difference

Imagine having the power to shape your destiny and create a life filled with purpose, passion, and positivity. That's what optimism can do for you! It's not just a feeling of being happy; it's a powerful tool that can propel you towards success and help you achieve your goals.

Your attitude is the key to releasing your full potential. It's the constant interplay of thought, action, and emotion that determines whether you see the glass half full or half empty. And the good news is that you have the power to choose your attitude!

It's often said, "How you do anything is how you do everything." This means that the way you operate is predictable – your approach is consistent across every area of life. Examining the smallest moments of your day reveals your attitude toward life. Your attitude shapes how life responds to you. Life treats you the way you allow it to.

If you approach life casually, you will perform tasks in an indifferent manner, leading to carelessness. Renowned motivational speaker Jim Rohn expressed it succinctly: *"Casualness leads to casualties."* A casual attitude toward health can cause setbacks; a relaxed approach to your job could lead to job loss. Avoid becoming a casualty. A positive attitude – a constructive, optimistic view of yourself and your work – amplifies success in every field, as illustrated in the following poem.

The Little Red Hen

Said the big white rooster, 'Gosh all Hemlock, things are tough,
Seems that worms are getting scarce and I cannot find enough.
What's become of all those fat ones is a mystery to me;
There were thousands through the rainy spell, but now where can they be?'

The little red hen, who heard him, didn't grumble or complain,
She had been through lots of dry spells, she had lived through floods of rain;

So she flew up on the grindstone and she gave her claws a
whet,
And she said, 'I've never seen a time there were no worms
to get.'

She picked a new and undug spot; the earth was hard and
firm.
The big white rooster jeered, 'New ground! That's no place
for a worm.'
The little red hen spread her feet, she dug fast and free,
'I must go to the worms,' she said, 'the worms won't come
to me.'

The rooster vainly spent his day, through habit by the ways,
Where fat worms have passed in squads, back in the rainy
days.
When nightfall found him supperless, he growled in
accents rough,
'I'm as hungry as a fowl can be. Conditions sure are tough.'

He turned to the little red hen and said, 'It's worse with
you,
For you're not only hungry, but you must be tired too.
I rested while I watched for worms, so I feel fairly perk;
But how are you? Without worms, too? And after all that
work?'

The little red hen hopped to her perch and dropped her
eyes to sleep,
And murmured, in a drowsy tone, 'Young man, hear this
and weep.
I'm full of worms and happy, for I've eaten like a pig;
The worms are there, but you must dig.'

~ Author unknown.

Your attitude is the secret sauce that determines how others respond to you, how you respond to challenges, and, inevitably, how successful you become. So, don't leave it to chance – choose your attitude! Choose to see the good in every situation, even the tough ones. Because every hardship offers a valuable lesson, and every challenge is an opportunity to grow.

High achievers know this secret. They understand that a positive attitude is the key to releasing their full potential. They believe that the best is yet to come, and they approach life with enthusiasm and optimism. And wherever you find people excelling and achieving outstanding results, you'll encounter individuals with a positive attitude.

But here's the amazing thing: research shows that a positive attitude is more important than intelligence when it comes to achieving success. Yes, you read that right – a positive attitude can trump intelligence! So, if you're someone who's struggled with self-doubt or negativity, don't worry – you can still achieve your goals.

The key is to embrace enthusiasm for life and approach your tasks with positivity. Enthusiasm is contagious, so make sure you're spreading the right kind. And don't be discouraged by setbacks – note that even the great inventor Thomas Edison maintained a positive mindset despite facing numerous failures.

Great Value in Disaster

Thomas Edison's laboratory was virtually destroyed by fire in December 1914. Although the damage exceeded $2 million, the buildings were only insured for $238,000 because they were made of concrete and thought to be fireproof.

Much of Edison's life's work went up in spectacular flames. Edison's 24-year-old son, Charles, frantically searched for his father and finally found him, calmly watching the scene, his face glowing in the reflection, his white hair blowing in the wind.

'My heart ached for him,' said Charles. 'He was 67 – no longer a young man – and everything was going up in flames. When he saw me, he shouted, "Charles, where's your mother?"'

When I told him I didn't know, he said, 'Find her. Bring her here. She will never see anything like this as long as she lives.'

The next morning, Edison looked at the ruins and said, 'There is great value in disaster. All our mistakes are burned up. Thank God we can start anew.'

Three weeks after the fire, Edison managed to deliver his first phonograph.

Life is truly an "inside job." As within, so without – your external world, the life you experience mirrors your inner world of thoughts and emotions. If you want to change your external experiences, change must begin internally. Regardless of your outer circumstances, you can always shift your inner world. Start by altering your attitude toward life, and life will reciprocate.

It's unfortunate that some dismiss the idea of 'finding opportunity in adversity' as overly optimistic. Yet, like Edison, if you slow down and look sincerely, you'll find it. Practice this mindset for 30 days, and you'll cultivate a lifelong habit that serves you well… guaranteed!

9.3   Be Patient…And Reap Greater Rewards

In our fast-moving world, we're often tempted to seek instant gratification. But true success is a marathon, not a sprint. It requires patience, perseverance, and the understanding that great rewards often come after a period of waiting. Such is the Law of Sowing and Reaping.

Consider nature. Farmers do not expect to plant seeds and harvest on the same day. Every outcome has a gestation period, a time of growth and development before it manifests into physical form. Carrots take seven weeks to grow, onions take nine weeks, human babies take 40 weeks to develop in the womb, and elephants take 22 months. Sometimes, no growth or development is visible for an extended period.

The Chinese bamboo plant shows no visible growth for the first four years. Imagine that – four full years! Then, in the fifth year, within just six weeks, the plant shoots up to an astonishing 30 meters! During those initial years, unseen and hidden from view, the plant produces deep, stabilizing roots to support its remarkable upward growth. The World Book Encyclopedia notes that a bamboo plant can grow one meter in a single 24-hour period.

Our life results often resemble the growth of the Chinese bamboo plant. There is a decisive period between initiating an endeavor and enjoying its returns. During this period, many become impatient, unable to see progress despite their efforts. They lose faith, give up, and declare, "It didn't work."

To succeed in any endeavor, acknowledge the wisdom of nature. We cannot simply plant a seed and expect immediate rewards. There is a natural progression of events from seeding to harvest, and this is how it works:

1. We will reap if we sow.
2. We reap what we sow.
3. We reap after we sow.
4. We reap more than we sow.

5. We must nurture what we have sown.
6. The most significant harvest usually requires the longest time to reach its reaping season.
7. We must be patient.

An Enlightened Thought for Reflection

Everything comes to him who hustles while he waits.

~ Thomas A. Edison

Patience is more than just waiting; it's a powerful strategy for success. It's about working hard, staying committed, and understanding that great things take time. Consider it an investment in your future – the more you put in now, the greater the rewards will be later.

Patience isn't just a virtue; it's an intelligent choice. It's about seeing the big picture, deciding to delay gratification, setting ambitious goals, and working towards them daily.

Those who persevere and keep working and waiting reap the greatest rewards. So, the next time you feel impatient, recognize that patience holds incredible potential.

Here's a simple verse that captures the essence of patience:

Let nothing disturb thee;
Let nothing dismay thee;
All things pass;
God never changes.
Patience attains
All that it strives for.

~ St. Teresa de Cepeda

9.4   Be Creative – Use Your Natural Gift

Creativity is a powerful force that can transform your life. It's not just for artists; it's the catalyst for progress, driving breakthroughs in technology, art, and science. By thinking creatively, you can uncover new possibilities and find more effective ways of doing things.

Creativity is your path to the future; all you need to do is unleash it. Don't let fear of the unconventional hold you back.   As Albert Einstein said:

If at first the idea is not absurd, then there is no hope for it.

But what holds us back from unleashing our creativity? Often, it's our tendency to think competitively rather than creatively.

We often waste energy competing by mimicking others in an attempt to outdo them. This competitive approach is weak; it requires someone to lose for you to win. Consider this scenario: If a pie is shared among four people, one person having more than a quarter means another must have less. This mindset creates a win-lose scenario, even if only in your mind. Instead, be creative. Make the pie bigger so everyone can have more. In business, this "pie" could represent the marketplace for a specific product or service.

Adopting a competitive mindset means you'll always be a follower, waiting for someone else to create something first so you can then copy their initiative. You don't need to take away from others to succeed. Cheating or exploiting others is not necessary. No wrong ever turns out right, and the law of Cause and Effect ensures any unfair gain is diminished. William Penn wisely stated:

What is wrong is wrong, even if everyone is doing it. Right is still right, even if no one else is doing it.

Learn from others, but don't compete by copying them. Differentiate yourself by adding value. Prosperity arises from creating value for others. The universe responds to the energy you emit, and competitive thinking often puts you at odds with the natural laws of the universe, which favor cooperation and creation. You are here to work in partnership with the universe. You are a co-creator, not a competitor.

You can achieve what you want, but in a way that benefits every other person affected by your actions, as illustrated in the following story.

Growing Good Corn

There was a Nebraska farmer who grew award-winning corn. Each year, he entered his corn in the state fair, where it won a blue ribbon.

One year, a newspaper reporter interviewed him and learned that the farmer had shared his seed corn with his neighbors.

'How can you afford to share your best seed corn with your neighbors when they enter corn in competition with yours each year?' the reporter asked.

'Why, sir,' said the farmer, 'didn't you know? The wind picks up pollen from the ripening corn and swirls it from field to field. If my neighbors grow inferior corn, cross-pollination will steadily degrade the quality of my corn. If I am to grow good corn, I must help my neighbors grow good corn.'

The farmer was very much aware of the connectedness of life. His corn could not improve unless his neighbor's corn also improved.

The same is true in other aspects of life. Those who choose to be at peace must help their neighbors to be at peace. Those who choose to live well must help others to live well, for the value of a life is measured by the lives it touches. And those who choose to be happy must help others to find happiness, for the welfare of each is bound up with the welfare of all.

The lesson for each of us is this: if we are to prosper, we must help others prosper.

Successful individuals are dedicated to creating value for others. They recognize that their rewards in life are directly proportional to the services they render. Generally, the most successful people are those who have helped the largest number of others achieve their desires. Sustainable success is not about survival of the fittest; it's about cooperation. It's the most fun too!

9.5   Be Tolerant and Understanding – It Cuts Both Ways

As social creatures, we constantly interact with others and often have judgmental feelings about everyone and everything we encounter. It's human nature to have biases, form opinions, and sometimes label others based on first impressions. Our judgments are rarely neutral; they may be positive or negative, often leading to misunderstandings and conflicts. These judgmental feelings stem from our ever-changing values, which are shaped by our personal life experiences.

Evaluating a situation is different from being judgmental. It's okay to make judgments, like when evaluating a job candidate's qualifications and experience. However, being judgmental means having a critical or harsh attitude toward others. We usually consider someone judgmental when they assign negative connotations or accuse others of wrongdoing.

Often, we judge others based on our perceptions of them – including their appearance, beliefs, preferences, mannerisms, choices, actions (or lack thereof), relationships, profession, academic qualifications, age, gender, and where they live. These judgments are mainly influenced by our own conditioning, which includes prejudices, ego, fear, jealousy, or ignorance, rather than wisdom and discernment.

We all have unique personalities, habits, and values shaped by our different cultures, societies, and countries of origin. Being judgmental because someone doesn't fit our definition of 'normal' is choosing to be narrow-minded instead of open-minded and understanding.

Sometimes, we judge people who don't conform to societal norms without considering why they act the way they do. Perhaps the person we judge has faced disadvantages – abuse, disorders, or trauma. We are all unique and traveling toward the same goal of self-realization. Some paths may be longer due to choices made, but no path is more or less important than another. The truth is, how you treat others is really a reflection of yourself. More importantly, the energy you emit always comes back to you.

An Enlightened Thought for Reflection

Remember that I'm Human. Before you judge me or decide how you'll deal with me, walk awhile in my shoes. If you do, I think you'll find with more understanding we can meet in the middle and walk the rest of the way together.

~ Eric Harvey and Steve Ventura

When you refrain from judging others, you can accept and appreciate their differences. Being tolerant of others helps you understand them better. American writer Ken Keyes Jr. said, *"A loving person lives in a loving world. A hostile person lives in a hostile world. Everyone you meet is your mirror."* This means that the way we treat others reflects how we feel about ourselves.

Author Ken Wilber also offers valuable advice: *"If you want to know what someone is really like, listen to what they say about other people."* This is because the things that bother us most about others are usually unrecognized aspects of ourselves.

An Enlightened Thought for Reflection

When you judge another, you do not define them;
you define yourself.

~ Wayne Dyer

Have you ever misjudged someone because of your own biases or lack of information? Sometimes, our actions can speak louder than words, revealing our true attitude towards others. This delightful poem tells the story of a woman who learns a valuable lesson about judging others too quickly.

The Cookie Thief

A woman was waiting at an airport one night
With several long hours before her flight
She hunted for a book in the airport shop
Bought a bag of cookies and found a place to drop
She was engrossed in her book but happened to see
That the man beside her, as bold as could be
Grabbed a cookie or two from the bag between
Which she tried to ignore to avoid a scene
She munched cookies and watched the clock
As this gutsy cookie thief diminished her stock
She was getting more irritated as the minutes ticked by
Thinking if I weren't so nice, I'd blacken his eye.
With each cookie she took, he took one too
And when only one was left, she wondered what he'd do.

He took the last cookie and broke it in half
He offered her half as he ate the other
She snatched it from him and thought, Oh, brother.
This guy has some nerve, and he's also rude.
Why, he didn't even show any gratitude.
She had never known when she had been so galled
And sighed with relief when her flight was called.
She gathered her belongings and headed for the gate
Refusing to look back at the thieving ingrate
She boarded the plane and sank in her seat
Then sought her book, which was almost complete.
As she reached in her baggage, she gasped with surprise.
There was her bag of cookies in front of her eyes
'If mine are here,' she moaned with despair
'Then the others were his, and he tried to share.'
Too late to apologize, she realized with grief
That she was the rude one, the ingrate, the thief.

~ Valerie Cox

Judging others is a harmful habit. The more entrenched it becomes, the harder it is to overcome. It's like a boomerang – what you throw out comes back to you. When we judge someone, we release negative energy that can hurt us in return.

To grow and succeed, we need to move beyond our habitual 'black-or-white' thinking (with no shades of grey) because this type of thinking limits us and holds us back. Instead, let's try to see things from different perspectives. Doing this allows us to open ourselves to new possibilities and achieve our goals.

9.6 Be a Go-Giver – It's a Paradox!

The process of manifesting success requires that you give and serve others. It's a Universal Law. You have to give before you get. You plant the seeds before you reap the harvest, and the more you sow, the more you reap. In fact, the law works to give you back more than you have sown. The giver's harvest is always abundant.

The great secret of giving is to give what you want to receive or what you desire the most. You attract what you give – the energy you emit from within you. If you emit love, respect, compassion, and understanding, it comes back to you. The universe gives back what you emit.

In giving to others, you will find yourself blessed. The simplest way to achieve your desires is by assisting others in achieving theirs. This concept was eloquently expressed by famed motivational speaker Zig Ziglar, who said, *"You can have anything you want in life if you will just help enough other people get what they want."*

An Enlightened Thought for Reflection

It is one of the most beautiful compensations of life that no man can sincerely try to help another without helping himself.

~Ralph Waldo Emerson

It's a shame that we often wait to receive before we give. This approach is like sitting in front of a fireplace and saying, 'Give me some heat, and then I'll give you some firewood.' Our conditioning leads us to seek abundance solely for ourselves. This approach is ineffective, at least not in the real sense of the word abundance. One can be financially rich, but morally or spiritually bankrupt, or lacking in fulfilling relationships with others.

The Law of Abundance allows you to attract as much abundance as you want by enriching others in various ways. The more lives you enrich, the greater your abundance. This powerful natural law of giving of ourselves will, in turn, give us much in return. This is one of the greatest secrets of life.

When you give, do so without apprehension or fear of loss, but with gratitude, love, and delight! The secret to giving lies in not caring about whether it will come back to you. Give without expecting anything in return; give because your heart moves you to give. Once you cease to care, you align with the Universe and the natural flow of life.

Don't treat giving as a negotiation with the Universe; it won't yield results. Your intention creates your results. Never give to receive intentionally. However, it is perfectly fine to give with the understanding that the Laws of the Universe will return the favor at some future date. Here is a powerful story that illustrates this principle.

The Power of Giving

It was a really hot summer's day many years ago. I was on my way to pick up two items at the grocery store. In those days, I was a frequent visitor to the supermarket because there never seemed to be enough money for a whole week's food-shopping at once.

You see, my young wife, after a tragic battle with cancer, had died just a few months earlier. There was no insurance, just many expenses and a mountain of bills. I held a part-time job, which barely generated enough money to feed my two young children.

Things were bad, really bad.

And so it was that day, with a heavy heart and four dollars in my pocket, I was on my way to the supermarket to purchase a gallon of milk and a loaf of bread. The children were hungry and I had to get them something to eat. As I came to a red traffic light, I noticed on my right a young man, a young woman, and a child on the grass next to the road. The blistering noonday sun beat down on them without mercy.

The man held up a cardboard sign which read, 'Will Work for Food.' The woman stood next to him. She just stared at the cars that stopped at the red light. The child, probably about two years old, sat on the grass holding a one-armed doll. I noticed all this in the thirty seconds it took for the traffic light to change to green.

I wanted so desperately to give them a few dollars, but if I did that, there wouldn't be enough left to buy the milk and bread. Four dollars will only go so far. As the light changed, I took one last glance at the three of them and sped off, feeling both guilty (for not helping them) and sad (because I didn't have enough money to share with them).

As I kept driving, I couldn't get the picture of the three of them out of my mind. The sad, haunting eyes of the young man and his family stayed with me for about a mile. I could take it no longer. I felt their pain and had to do something about it. I turned around and drove back to where I had last seen them.

I pulled up close to them and handed the man two of my four dollars. There were tears in his eyes as he thanked me. I smiled and drove on to the supermarket. Perhaps both milk and bread would be on sale, I thought. And what if I only got milk alone, or just the bread? Well, it would have to do.

I pulled into the parking lot, still thinking about the whole incident, yet feeling good about what I had done. As I stepped out of the car, my foot slid on something on the pavement. There by my feet was a twenty-dollar bill. I just couldn't believe it. I looked all around, picked it up with awe, went into the store, and purchased not only bread and milk but several other items I desperately needed.

I never forgot that incident. It reminded me that the universe was strange and mysterious. It confirmed my belief that you could never out-give the universe. I gave away two dollars and got twenty in return. On my way back from the supermarket, I drove by the hungry family and shared five additional dollars with them.

This incident is only one of many that have occurred in my life.

It seems that the more we give, the more we get. It is, perhaps, one of those universal laws that say, 'If you want to receive, you must first give.'

~ John Harricharan

John Harricharan's story is a compelling illustration of how altruistic actions can result in unforeseen benefits. Some might argue that finding the twenty-dollar bill was mere coincidence or luck. Far from it. It was the perfect application of the Law of Giving at that moment. Despite his financial stress, John gave away half his remaining cash to a needy family. The subtlety of this law lies in his selfless act of giving precisely what he needed most at that moment – money!

Consider this: In a similar situation, would you act as John did?

An Enlightened Thought for Reflection

No one has ever become poor by giving.

~ Anne Frank

Everyone has something to share: a kind gesture, a compliment, or a simple smile. Even those who are most disadvantaged can feel the impact of kindness and generosity offered without conditions. There is divinity within us all. The Lord Buddha said:

If you knew what I know about the power of giving, you would not let a single meal pass without sharing it in some way.

Practice the gift of giving. Give to those in need with the intention of serving them for their sake, not yours. Give anonymously, keeping your generosity to yourself, as broadcasting it diminishes its impact in the Universe. Charity without fanfare or recognition is the highest form of charity. Besides, the joy that comes from knowing you've made a positive impact is frequently more fulfilling than any recognition you might get.

When giving, ensure the recipient doesn't feel ashamed or belittled. And never regret your decision to give – give with a good heart and be grateful for the opportunity.

Giving selflessly can also have a surprising benefit: it can bring abundance into your own life. When you give selflessly, you open yourself up to receiving more. Selflessness invites reciprocity; energy returns to its source multiplied!

Basic rhymes and sayings can sometimes express deep truths about the go-giver mindset. Reflect on the following rhyme:

A man there was, and they called him mad,
The more he gave, the more he had.

It's a potent reminder that generosity and abundance are inextricably linked.

The Vacuum Theory of Prosperity

There's a concept called the "vacuum theory of prosperity" that suggests that when you create a space or situation, nature will fill it. The following narrative illustrates this idea:

The Tale of Two Seas

The Sea of Galilee and the Dead Sea are made of the same water.
It flows down, clean and cool, from the heights of Herman and the roots of the cedars of Lebanon.
The Sea of Galilee makes beauty of it,
for the Sea of Galilee has an outlet. It gets to give.
It gathers in its riches that it may pour them out again
to fertilize the Jordan plain.
But the Dead Sea with the same water makes horror.
For the Dead Sea has no outlet. It gets to keep.

~ Harry Emerson Fosdick (excerpt from 'The Meaning Of Service')

Mother Nature teaches us valuable lessons. Sharing what you have with others creates a cycle of giving and receiving that leads to abundance for everyone involved.

Clear out your personal spaces of old or unused items. They create clutter and negative energy. Let them go. Donate these things to charity or give them to someone who needs them.

Understand that the universe doesn't like empty spaces, and clearing out unused items will create a space for new, fresh things to enter your life. Similarly, if you don't give, the universe won't give back to you. Contemplate this daily.

Tithing: Giving Back and Getting More

Tithing is a great way to give back. It means donating a part of your income to charities or causes you believe in. Tithing has been used for a long time and is still recommended by many people, including religious leaders and business owners.

By giving a portion of your money to others, you form a habit of generosity. This can attract prosperity into your life.

Many successful people and businesses tithe as part of their financial plan. It helps those who are less fortunate and reminds us that there's always enough to share.

Be a Giver

Being a giver means always looking for ways to help others. Notice the needs around you and offer help whenever you can. Giving is essential, whether at work, volunteering, or supporting a cause you care about.

It is said, *"It is in giving, not in getting, that our lives are blest."* This sentiment rings true! In giving, we attain more.

Make giving a habit. Choose to be a go-giver, more so than being a go-getter. Include acts of kindness in your daily routine. Over time, giving will become natural.

9.7   Be Responsible...and 'Do Something'

Taking responsibility for your actions and your life is essential for a meaningful and prosperous existence. It means recognizing that you have control over your choices and that these choices lead to specific outcomes. If you don't take charge, someone else will.

When you take charge, you actively shape your life instead of letting events happen to you. You create opportunities instead of waiting for them to appear. Understand that no one is coming to save you.

In times of turmoil, it's natural to feel powerless. But, you always have the power to choose how to respond. Consider this story:

Do Something

In the depths of despair, a man, overwhelmed by the relentless tide of pain and suffering surrounding him, collapsed to his knees and pounded the earth in frustration.

With tear-streaked cheeks turned towards the heavens, he unleashed a desperate cry to his God.

"Behold this chaos! Witness the agony and torment, the bloodshed and malice! Oh God, why do you remain silent? *Why don't you do something?*"

And in that moment of anguish, a divine whisper pierced the darkness, reaching the depths of his soul.

"I have," spoke the voice, gentle yet resolute. "I sent you."

~ Anonymous

This story embodies a profound truth: we all have a role in shaping our world. We can complain about injustice, or choose to be part of the solution. The choice is ours.

Your circumstances do not define you; your attitude, choices, and actions shape who you are. If you want something to change, take steps to make it happen.

Taking personal responsibility is one of the most important things you can do for yourself. If you fail to do so, you give away your power and lose control over your life. While you can relinquish control over your life, you cannot relinquish personal responsibility. No matter how you try to avoid responsibility, it's always there, whether you like it or not.

You will only feel good about yourself to the extent that you take control of your life. Ironically, many of us give up this control, the very thing

138

that makes us feel good about ourselves. We then blame circumstances, others, or "bad luck" for our situations.

Let's be honest – taking responsibility isn't always easy, but it is empowering. It means facing your mistakes head-on, owning your decisions (good and bad), and accepting that your choices shape your reality. By accepting responsibility, you unlock your potential for change and pave the way for a more fulfilling life.

Successful people understand this. They create the life they want by taking charge, refusing to play the blame game, or making excuses. Their mindset is: "*If it's to be, it's up to me.*" This mindset is life-changing, transforming you from a passive observer of your life to its active creator.

Accepting responsibility is like turning on a light in a dark room. Suddenly, you see paths and possibilities that were always there but hidden in the shadows. It's a pivotal moment, a turning point that has launched countless success stories throughout history.

Is it challenging? Absolutely. It requires self-awareness, courage, and a willingness to grow. You'll face uncomfortable truths and daunting obstacles. But the rewards are immeasurable – a life of purpose, achievement, and fulfillment.

9.8   Be Forgiving…and Experience the Freedom

Forgiveness is a powerful way to create abundance in your life, even though it may not seem like it. It is essential to forgive yourself and others. Forgiveness means acknowledging past errors, whether yours or someone else's. It's a decision to make amends with someone you've hurt or who has hurt you, releasing feelings of guilt or anger.

Most individuals, whether consciously or subconsciously, may cause harm to others in both significant and minor ways at some point. We are all in a constant state of learning and growth, which is why we all require forgiveness.

Sometimes, we unknowingly create situations that lead to our own pain by allowing others to take advantage of us. This can stem from our actions or inaction; it might be something we've done to provoke a response, or simply being quiet or submissive. Regardless of the reason, it's essential to forgive both ourselves and those who have caused us pain.

No one is perfect; we all make mistakes. Most people find it much harder to forgive themselves than to forgive others. Letting go of guilt for past mistakes can feel nearly impossible. By holding onto this guilt, sadness, and pain, we unnecessarily relive distressing events.

Release the self-guilt. You deserve to be happy and live in joy. In this state, you will attract more positivity into your life. Besides, you are equally worthy and deserving of forgiveness.

An Enlightened Thought for Reflection

The weak can never forgive. Forgiveness is the attribute of the strong.

~ *Mahatma Gandhi*

The Consequences of Non-forgiveness

Forgiveness does not occur naturally; it is a conscious choice. You don't have to forgive, but holding onto hurt is detrimental to your mental and physical health. It affects your vibrational state. If you harbor hatred toward someone, you also suffer from that hatred. Numerous medical studies connect unresolved anger to illness.

The Buddha stated, *"You will not be punished* for *your anger; you will be punished* by *your anger."* When you're angry, your body can react by increasing acid production in the stomach. This can lead to inflammation, causing symptoms such as upper abdominal pain, heartburn, indigestion, nausea, and other discomfort. In some cases, the burning sensation in

140

the stomach can become constant, possibly leading to bleeding in the stomach lining.

Anger is a negative emotion that produces adverse outcomes in our lives. Author Ken Keyes observed:

> *The world tends to be your mirror. A peaceful person lives in a peaceful world. An angry person creates an angry world... An unfriendly person should not be surprised when he/she meets only unfriendly people.*

Our lack of forgiveness invites more circumstances that feed our anger and reinforce feelings of victimization. Choosing not to forgive means choosing to remain a victim. Non-forgiveness binds you to the person who caused your hurt. Holding onto anger, resentment, and grudges poisons your body with toxins and weakens your immune system.

An Enlightened Thought for Reflection

By far the strongest poison to the human spirit is the inability to forgive oneself or another person... Forgiving does not mean saying that what happened to you doesn't matter, or that it is alright for someone to have violated you. It simply means releasing the negative feelings you have about that event and the person or persons involved.

~ Caroline Myss

The Need to Forgive

To experience emotional healing and let in new, brighter feelings, you've got to forgive. Forgiveness is not an option but a necessary step towards healing. It's something that happens inside you – it's personal. You can forgive someone without even telling them.

Forgiving others can be challenging, but it's essential for breaking free from the victim mindset. Living with forgiveness at the core of your being is non-negotiable if you're aiming to expand your consciousness. Forgiveness occurs at the spiritual level, while forgetting happens at the mental level. The two aren't the same, nor do they need to be – forgiving does not require forgetting.

When hesitant about forgiving someone for a wrongful act, recall Scottish philosopher Thomas Carlyle's words: *"A great man shows his greatness by the way he treats little men."* Aim to be a great individual. Forgiveness isn't just about the other person; it's about who you become in the process – stronger, yes, but also softer in the ways that matter.

An Enlightened Thought for Reflection

Anger makes you smaller,
while forgiveness forces you to grow beyond what you were.

~ Cherie Carter-Scott

Forgiveness primarily benefits you rather than the other person. In forgiving, you process feelings of pain, grief, and anger, freeing yourself from the hurt inflicted by others and your own mistakes. When you choose to forgive, you choose to live in the present rather than dwelling on the past; you're intentionally creating the kind of life you want, both in this moment and in the future.

How to Forgive

Forgiveness does not mean condoning negative or inappropriate behavior, nor does it require reconciling with those who mistreat you. It means acknowledging that someone has hurt you and choosing to grant them mercy.

You can forgive without excusing the act. Forgiveness doesn't negate your right to seek restitution. If someone has harmed you, you have the right to pursue ethical and legal remedies – that's justice, not vengeance.

The only people worth "getting even" with are those who've lifted you up or shown you kindness. Match their goodness, not the harm done by others.

An Enlightened Thought for Reflection

There is no revenge so complete as forgiveness.

~ Josh Billings

When thoughts of past hurts arise, dismiss them with, "No, thank you. I have decided to move on rather than be constrained by you. I have better things to do; I'll focus on what is good in my life and the goals I want to accomplish." Alexander Pope wisely stated, *"To err is human; to forgive, divine."* Realize, you are divine.

Here is a beautiful poem that encapsulates the practice of forgiveness:

Forgiveness

If you try to reach inside of your heart
you can find forgiveness, or at least the start
And from that place where you can forgive
is where Hope, and Love, also thrive and live

And with each step that you try to take
and with that chance that your heart might break
Comes so much happiness, and so much strength
which Alone can carry you a fantastic length

For hate and anger will not get you there
and though you say that you just don't care
You can EASILY avoid the pain on which hate feeds
. . . the kind of hurt that No one needs

Just make the move, take that first stride
let go of the thing known as "Foolish Pride"
Maybe then you can start to repair the past
into something strong, that will mend, and last!

~ Barry S. Maltese

Remember, your present doesn't have to be your future, no matter your circumstances.

9.9   Be Faithful…and Swing Things in Your Favor

Faith is believing in something you can't see or prove, yet you know it's real or true. It's your willingness to wholeheartedly trust and rely on Universal Consciousness or God.

We are all connected to Universal Consciousness. Recognizing this connection is like inviting a higher power to join your team, even if it's just you and the universe. As Frederick Douglass once said, "*One and God make a majority.*" This is a profound insight – ultimately, the 'majority' rules or wins! Therefore, with this divine partnership, you can swing things in your favor and achieve almost anything you set your mind to.

To get the universe on your side, you need to have faith. Faith is shown through prayer and how you chase what you're dreaming of. Prayer is like sending a signal out into the cosmos, but the energy behind it – your determination, your action – is what powers it. Faith isn't just wishing; it's the fuel that turns intentions into answers. Faith heals, creates, saves, proclaims, preserves, dares, and inspires. Faith accomplishes everything – even the seemingly impossible.

Faith, mighty faith
The promise sees

And looks to God alone,
Laughs at impossibilities
And cries, 'It shall be done.'

~ Anonymous

You will receive from God according to your faith – not your faith while contemplating desires, but your faith while *actively working* to achieve them.

Your specific needs and circumstances do not move God as much as faith does. God responds to audacious, unashamed faith. Just as a small flame produces little light, little faith produces meager results. If you lack faith and still seek miraculous outcomes, you are fooling yourself. It simply won't work. When it comes to trusting God, you either have faith or don't. The following parable illustrates the point.

A Lesson in Faith and Trust

Fueled by a desire for solo glory, an ambitious mountain climber embarked on a perilous ascent. As dusk painted the sky, he neared the summit, his determination battling the encroaching darkness.

Tragically, a misstep sent him plummeting down the rocky slopes. His life flashed before him in those agonizing moments, the chilling realization of imminent death settling in.

Suddenly, a jolt halted his descent. He dangled precariously, suspended by a safety rope. In desperation, a prayer escaped his lips, pleading for divine intervention. A powerful voice boomed from above, echoing through the vastness: *"What would you have me do?"*

"Save me!" the climber cried out, his voice laced with urgency.

"Do you truly believe I can?" the voice queried.

"Of course, my Lord!" he affirmed; his faith seemingly unflinching.

Then came the unexpected instruction: *"Cut the rope if you wish to be saved."*

Silence descended, thick and heavy. The climber, caught in a web of fear and doubt, clung desperately to the very lifeline he was instructed to sever.

The following morning, a rescue team found the climber frozen to death, his hands still gripping the rope mere inches above the ground.

The narrative shows that faith often involves risk-taking and trusting what you can't see. It's about casting aside fear and doubt and stepping into the unknown with courage.

A life of faith is fundamentally a life of risk. Demonstrating faith in life is not for the faint-hearted or those content to play it safe. As the beautiful poem by Nancy Spiegelberg illustrates, faith flourishes when we stop playing small; when we abandon our small cup and approach God with a bucket:

Lord, I crawled across the barrenness To You
With my empty cup,
Uncertain in asking
Any small drop of refreshment.
If only I had known You better,
I'd have come running
With a bucket.

Pray With Gratitude

In his book, *Secrets of the Lost Mode of Prayer*, bestselling author Gregg Braden shares a remarkable story about a Native American friend, David, who took him on a quest to bring rain during an extended drought in New Mexico in the 1990s. Here is that story:

> The pair had walked quite a distance to a sacred place used by David's ancestors for prayer and ritual. David took off his shoes and stepped into the circle. He acknowledged the four directions and his ancestors, placed his hands in prayer position, closed his eyes, and then stood motionless in silence.
>
> After a few moments, he said he had finished and was ready to leave.
>
> Gregg, waiting for something more elaborate to happen, said, *"I thought you were going to pray for rain."*
>
> *"No,"* he replied. *"I said that I would pray rain. If I had prayed for rain, it could never happen."*
>
> When Gregg asked him why, he said, *"It's because the moment you pray for something to occur, you've just acknowledged that it's not existing in that moment – and you may actually be denying the very thing you'd like to bring forward in your prayers."*
>
> He described how the elders of his village had shared the secrets of prayer with him when he was a young boy. The key, he said, is that when we ask for something to happen, we give power to what we do not have.
>
> *"If you pray for rain, you affirm the lack of what you want and you, therefore, create more lack of what you want – in this case, rain. When you pray rain [instead of pray for rain], you affirm the existence of rain right now, right here, in this moment. You offer gratitude for what you already have or expect to have,"* he explained.

"Well, if you didn't pray for rain just now when you closed your eyes, what did you do?" asked Gregg.

He said, *"When I closed my eyes, I felt the feeling of what it feels like after there's been so much rain that I can stand with my naked feet in the mud of my pueblo village. I smelled the smells of rainwater rolling off the earthen walls of our homes. And I felt what it feels like to walk through a field of corn that is chest high because of all the rain that has fallen. In that way, I plant a seed for the possibility of that rain, and then I give thanks of gratitude and appreciation."*

"You mean gratitude for the rain that you've created?" asked Gregg.

And he said, *"No, we don't create the rain. I'm giving thanks of gratitude and appreciation for the opportunity to commune with the forces of creation."*

As the story goes, it did indeed rain thereafter.

FEELING is the Prayer – Gregg Braden Quotes

According to Gregg Braden, the lost mode of prayer is based solely on feeling. During a pilgrimage to the Tibetan plateau monasteries, through their translator, Braden asked the abbot of a monastery the same question that he'd asked each monk and nun they had met throughout their pilgrimage.

When we see your prayers, what are you doing? When we see you intone and chant for 14 and 16 hours a day, when we see the bells, the bowls, the gongs, the chimes, the mudras and the mantras on the outside, what is happening to you on the inside?

As the translator shared the abbot's reply, a powerful sensation rippled through Braden's body, and he knew that this was the reason they'd come to this place. The abbot replied:

"You have never seen our prayers because a prayer cannot be seen. What you have seen is what we do to create the feeling in our bodies. Feeling is the prayer!"

Braden says that rather than the sense of helplessness that often leads us to ask for assistance from a higher power, feeling-based prayer acknowledges our ability to communicate with God. This is the key – this is profound! Here is how Braden elaborates on the concept of feeling-based prayer.

"Without any words, without our hands held in a certain position or any outward physical expression, this mode of prayer simply invites us to feel a clear and powerful feeling as if our prayers have already been answered. Through this intangible 'language,' we participate in the healing of our bodies, the abundance that comes to our friends and families, and the peace between nations."

We are always feeling in each moment of every day of our lives. While we may not always be aware of just what we're feeling, we are feeling nonetheless. If feeling is the prayer and we're always feeling, then that means we're always in a state of prayer. Each moment is a prayer.

Life is a prayer! We're always sending a message to the mirror of creation, signaling healing or disease, peace or war, honoring or dishonoring our relationships with those we love. 'Life' is the Mind of God sending back to us what we feel – what we've prayed.

Change How You Pray Pray

Instead of complaining prayers don't work, change how you pray. Stop asking for what you want and need; express gratitude to God for prayers already answered. Don't be disappointed if the outcome isn't exactly what you envisioned; appreciate that God knows what you truly need.

Here is a beautiful poem to encapsulate this idea.

Prayer

I asked for strength, and God gave me difficulties to make me strong
I asked for wisdom, and God gave me problems to solve
I asked for prosperity, and God gave me brawn and brains to work
I asked for courage, and God gave me danger to overcome
I asked for patience, and God placed me in situations where I was forced to wait
I asked for love, and God gave me troubled people to help
I asked for favors and God gave me opportunities
I received nothing I wanted
I received everything I needed
My Prayer Has Been Answered.

~ Anonymous

If life is a prayer, and prayer is a feeling, then it goes without saying that *life itself is a feeling*. The 'feeling' described in this manner is really the intensity of our aura or the 'vibes' we put out. Since life is based on feelings, you constantly attract according to your emotional state. When you become emotionally charged about a particular goal, you emit a stronger vibration, and the stronger the vibration, the more rapidly you attract it into your life.

So, how do you evoke this feeling for your desired outcome?

Demonstrate faith – faith in yourself and your invisible partner. Act as if it is impossible to fail! Start acting like a success before you become one. Consider this: If you had already achieved your dream, how would you carry yourself? For example, would you dress smartly or shabbily? Would you walk confidently, with your head held high, or with a more subdued demeanor? Would you shake hands boldly or timidly? Would you exude self-assurance and trust?

In acting as if you have already succeeded, use all your senses – sight, sound, taste, smell, and touch – and experience the emotions tied to achieving your desired outcome. Remember, emotion is the language through which you communicate with the Universe. It would help if you genuinely felt every emotion triggered by your senses. Every cell in your body and every fiber of your being must resonate with your desired outcome in its completed form.

Do these things now. Act the part, and the Universe will match you step-by-step! Your results will reflect your faith!

9.10   Be Grateful… Because Whatever You Appreciate, Appreciates!

Faith and gratitude are powerfully interconnected. Faith begins with gratitude, according to author Wallace D. Wattles:

> *Faith is born of gratitude. The grateful mind continually expects good things, and expectation becomes faith… The person who can sincerely thank God for the things which, as yet he owns only in imagination, has real faith. …He will cause the creation of whatever he wants.*

Be grateful. Count your blessings. You have much to appreciate. Thankfulness for what you have is fundamental to your well-being and happiness. Here's an emotive poem to help you recognize some of your many blessings:

Forgive Me When I Whine

Today, upon a bus,
I saw a lovely girl with golden hair.
I envied her.

She seemed so happy;
I wished I were as fair.
When suddenly she rose to leave,
I saw her hobble down the aisle;
She had one leg and wore a crutch;
But as she passed... a smile!
Oh, God forgive me when I whine,
I have two legs.
The world is mine!

I stopped to buy some candy.
The lad who sold it had such charm.
I talked with him.
He seemed so glad.
If I were late it would do no harm.
And as I left he said to me,
'I thank you; you have been so kind.
It's nice to talk with folks like you.
You see,' he said, "I'm blind.'
Oh, God forgive me when I whine,
I have two eyes. The world is mine!

Later, while walking down the street,
I saw a child with eyes of blue.
He stood and watched the others play.
He did not know what to do.
I stopped a moment; then I said,
'Why don't you join the others, dear?'
He looked ahead without a word,
And then I knew he could not hear.
Oh, God forgive me when I whine,
I have two ears.
The world is mine!

With feet to take me where I'd go,
With eyes to see the sunset's glow,

With ears to hear what I would know...
Oh, God forgive me when I whine.
I'm blessed indeed.
The world is mine!

~ Red Foley

Gratitude is the expression of thankfulness for what you have. Grateful individuals tend to be happier than others. This does not mean they have everything they want, but they choose to accept their current circumstances with gratitude and contentment.

Many different techniques can be used to nurture an attitude of gratitude. It is important to practice consistently, ideally at the same time each day, to form a habit. Keeping a gratitude journal is a popular method – each day, list five to ten things for which you are thankful.

Another helpful technique is to sit silently and reflect each day. Start and end your day with gratitude. Wake up each morning with a thankful heart. Appreciate all the good in your life – past, present, and future. Give thanks for each new day, your life, your loved ones, and all your blessings. This spirit of gratitude sets a positive tone for the day, helping you recognize challenges as opportunities rather than problems. Again, before bedtime, express gratitude for the day you've just experienced.

But gratitude isn't just a feel-good exercise; it's a magnetic force. It connects you with Universal Consciousness and opens the flow of blessings. This is a powerful realization: when you practice gratitude, your energy transforms. It's as if you're tuning into a higher frequency that effortlessly attracts abundance and opportunities. Embrace this truth, and watch how it positively impacts your life.

An Enlightened Thought for Reflection

You cannot exercise much power without gratitude because it is gratitude that keeps you connected with [Cosmic] power.

~ Wallace D. Wattles

The most potent key to creation is thankfulness in advance. Here's an excerpt from the book *Conversations with God*, emphasizing the importance of saying "Thank You" ahead of time:

> *This place of knowing is a place of intense and incredible gratitude. It is thankfulness in advance. And that, perhaps, is the biggest key to creation: to be grateful before, and for, the creation. Such taking for granted is not only condoned but encouraged. It is the sure sign of mastery. All Masters know in advance that the deed has been done.*

UN Ambassador for world peace James Twyman articulated his perspective:

> *When we ask for something to happen, the attention is on the fact that we don't have it now. But when we feel that it has already occurred, then we put out an energy that actually draws that reality to us. Gratitude is a key element. It is very important to be grateful.*

It's no coincidence that throughout history, wise leaders and thinkers practiced gratitude *in advance* of receiving what they wanted. Why? Because it engenders confident expectancy – a deep belief that what you desire is already yours. And according to the Law of Attraction, that's the key. To draw something into your life, you must embody the feeling of already having it.

When you consciously acknowledge and express gratitude for your blessings, you emit positive emotional energy. Gratitude is an emotion, and emotion is energy. Since gratitude radiates positive energy, it attracts favorable conditions into your life. Feeling joy and anticipation for something you want before receiving it sets you in perfect harmony with the Universe's flow, making manifestation a natural process. The emotion of joy attracts joyful circumstances. What you appreciate, appreciates – whatever you are thankful for expands, whether it's love, opportunities, or abundance.

Challenges, though, are gratitude's sneaky little tests. Be grateful for them because they are really growth opportunities in disguise. When you view challenges with gratitude, they stop being problems and start becoming teachers, showing you where to evolve or shift course. That doesn't mean you ignore dissatisfaction – it just means you use it as fuel for change, rather than letting it drag you into negativity… as the following poem illustrates:

Be Thankful

Be thankful that you don't already have everything you desire.
If you did, what would there be to look forward to?
Be thankful when you don't know something,
for it gives you the opportunity to learn.
Be thankful for the difficult times.
During those times you grow.
Be thankful for your limitations,
because they give you opportunities for improvement.
Be thankful for each new challenge,
because it will build your strength and character.
Be thankful for your mistakes.
They will teach you valuable lessons.
Be thankful when you're tired and weary,
because it means you've made a difference.
It's easy to be thankful for the good things.
A life of rich fulfillment comes to those who
are also thankful for the setbacks.
Gratitude can turn a negative into a positive.
Find a way to be thankful for your troubles,
and they can become your blessings.

~ Anonymous

Studies have shown that deliberately practicing gratitude boosts your mood, energy, and even empathy. Gratitude isn't just a private feeling; it's social, too. It can show up in everyday actions, creating tangible results, as shown in the following story.

In New York City, just fifteen yards from another stand, a particular newspaper vendor consistently outsold its neighbor by as much as four times. The secret? Gratitude. After every sale, the owner of the thriving stand offered a simple yet powerful expression: "Thank you." This genuine gratitude drew customers in, willing to go out of their way to patronize a stand where they felt recognized and valued.

So, how do you harness this universal law? Practice it consistently. Show appreciation to others – a note, a call, a moment of acknowledgment. Focus on the blessings you already have, but don't be afraid to express gratitude for what's still unfolding. By doing so, you align with the energy of abundance, and before you know it, gratitude becomes second nature – a powerful, life-changing force.

Having learned the key virtues and attitudes you must embody to 'BE a Better You,' it's time to continue your journey of conscious creation. Next, we examine how you should 'DO Your Part' to align yourself with your desire for a fulfilling life.

Hidden truths:

1. Successful people are committed to lifelong learning.
2. Life is an 'inside job' – the life you experience mirrors your inner world of thoughts and emotions.
3. Everything comes to him who hustles while he waits.
4. Sustainable success is not survival of the fittest; it is about survival of the most cooperative.

5. When you judge another, you do not define them; you define yourself.

6. The great secret of giving is to give what you want to receive or that which you want most.

7. You can give away control over your life, but you cannot give away responsibility.

8. Forgiveness is not an option, but a necessity for healing.

9. You will receive from God according to your faith.

10. Gratitude is a channel for receiving God's blessings.

Chapter 10

Do Your Part

The Law of Being and the Law of Doing are inextricably connected. While some believe you don't need to 'do' anything but simply allow your desired outcome to manifest, the reality is that you are a co-creator in the process. Even something as simple as being open to another person's perspective plays a role.

What you need to do depends on your specific goals. It will require varying amounts of energy, time, effort, or financial resources. Simply asking and waiting isn't enough. The Universe is your partner, but partnerships require participation. Be willing to burn up the necessary energy to manifest your desires. When you do your part, you can rest assured that the Universe will support you in achieving your goals.

To achieve your desires, you must change your vibrational state and raise your consciousness through various actions.

Let's explore the key things you need to 'DO' to achieve your desired outcomes.

10.1 Plan Your Work and Work Your Plan

To turn dreams into reality, you need a clear direction and a plan to get there. You can either proceed haphazardly or take a disciplined approach by planning your work and diligently following that plan. Though it requires initial effort, this disciplined approach saves time and provides a roadmap to your desired outcome. Here are the main processes to chart your journey and avoid pitfalls:

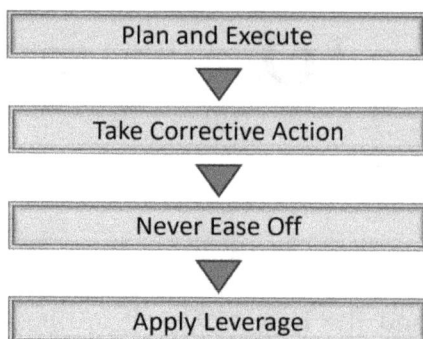

Let's examine each step in the progression.

10.1.1 Plan and Execute

Bears Kaufman once observed:

> Some of us create the future; some of us just let it happen. Others turn around and wonder, 'What happened?'

The difference lies in execution. A goal without a plan is like trying to build a house with no blueprint. It's not enough to fantasize or jot down ideas – you need a detailed action plan and the discipline to follow through.

An action plan is your roadmap from where you are now (Point A) to where you want to go (Point B). It can be a simple to-do list or an intricate project plan. Unfortunately, many skip this step, assuming things will magically fall into place – and they rarely do.

Most people make elaborate plans for a holiday or their wedding but have absolutely no plans for their lives. They live from one day to the next, expecting things to somehow magically change for the better. So, it's not surprising that most people are frustrated by their lack of accomplishment. Success requires treating your life goals with the same care and commitment you'd give to a big event.

Steps to Plan Effectively

1. Clearly define your desired outcome.
2. List the activities required to achieve it.
3. Sequence tasks logically, noting those that can happen simultaneously.
4. Assign realistic timelines for each activity.
5. Identify resources and support needed.
6. Recruit a team or helpers if necessary.
7. Take action.

It's really that simple!

An Enlightened Thought for Reflection

The secret of getting ahead is getting started. The secret of getting started is breaking your complex, overwhelming tasks into small manageable tasks, and then starting on the first one.

~ Mark Twain

Planning saves time, dramatically increasing productivity. An action plan clarifies your vision so you see the connection between the bigger picture and the next step. It is important to know what the bigger picture is like while at the same time, focusing on the moment and taking the next step forward. Professional tennis players keep their eye on the championship prize (the big picture), knowing that every shot and every point counts, even early on in the game. Similarly, it's essential that you make every action count and then continue to build on it.

The best plans in the world won't work until you take action. There is no such thing as 'something for nothing.' Plans represent intentions, but don't make activities happen – you do. Therefore, take bold action with commitment.

An Enlightened Thought for Reflection

Whatever you do, do with all your might, for things done by halves are never done right.

~ McGuffey Reader

Importantly, don't let what you *can't* do at present interfere with what you *can*.

As writer Kathleen Norris advised,

> *Before you begin a thing, remind yourself that difficulties and delays quite impossible to foresee are ahead. You can only see one thing clearly, and that is your goal. Form a mental vision of that and cling to it through thick and thin.*

Without doubt, there will be challenges, some big enough to scare you into giving up on your goals. This is the time to maintain your focus and stay the course, taking consistent daily action. Understand that action conquers fear. Each step forward will boost your confidence and self-esteem, guiding you closer to your goals.

Apply the 80/20 Rule (the Pareto Principle), which states that 80% of results come from 20% of our resources (including time and people). For example, a retail business might find that 20% of its customers account for 80% of its profits while the remaining 80% account for just 20%. It's wise for administrators to focus resources on that 20%.

In your plans, constantly ask yourself: What 20% of activities lead to 80% of results? Once you identify these activities, focus on them and optimize the remaining 80%. This may involve delegating, outsourcing, or even eliminating non-critical tasks to focus on what truly matters.

10.1.2   Take Corrective Action

As you chase your goals, keep a close eye on both your actions and their outcomes. Pay attention to what's working and what isn't. You'll receive feedback and signals telling you when you are off course and when course corrections are necessary.

Feedback is your greatest ally. It's not just information; it's a mirror showing you what's effective and what needs rethinking. Champions are made through this process – they listen, adjust, and improve based on what they learn.

An Enlightened Thought for Reflection

Feedback is the breakfast of champions.

~ Ken Blanchard

The road to success is rarely straight but rather a series of approximations and course adjustments. As you progress towards your goals, you'll experience some setbacks that will take you off course. NASA's moon mission spacecraft was only on course 3% of the time, making corrections 97% of the time. Yet it reached its target and accomplished what was to be the first successful manned moon landing. Similarly, your success depends on your willingness to adjust and get back on course.

Without feedback and adjustments, reaching your goals becomes a long and arduous journey. Challenges are an inherent part of pursuing your aspirations. They provide invaluable lessons that improve your character and boost your skills. Embracing and overcoming these obstacles is indispensable. Trying to bypass the learning process can impede your growth and prevent you from reaching your full potential, as illustrated by the following parable.

The Parable of the Butterfly

A kindhearted man discovered a butterfly cocoon and, moved by curiosity, watched the creature struggling to emerge through the tiny opening. After hours of watching the butterfly's effort, the man, driven by compassion, decided to help. He gently cut away the remaining cocoon, allowing the butterfly to escape effortlessly.

However, instead of a graceful, flying butterfly, the creature emerged with a swollen body and underdeveloped wings. The man hoped the wings would expand and lift the butterfly into the air, but his hopes were in vain. Having missed the crucial struggle, the butterfly's wings were too weak to support it in flight. As a result, the butterfly spent its short life crawling with a swollen body and shriveled wings.

This parable is a powerful reminder that growth often comes from overcoming challenges. Though seemingly painful, the butterfly's struggle within the cocoon served a necessary purpose. Each attempt to push through the barrier strengthened its wings, preparing it for the moment of flight.

Just as the butterfly needed its struggle to gain the strength to fly, sometimes we need to 'struggle' to break through the 'cocoons' of our lives to prepare for our evolutionary journey. Rather than seeing challenges as negative experiences, view them as opportunities for growth and evolution. Each challenge you face brings you closer to your goals, equipping you with new insights and abilities to tackle the next phase of your journey.

The Universe will continuously present learning experiences tailored to your specific needs. Embrace each experience with openness and a willingness to learn. If you don't grasp the wisdom it imparts, the lesson will repeat until you "get it."

10.1.3   Never Ease Off

Consistency is the bedrock of success. When you slack off or decelerate, you sacrifice precious momentum. As the adage goes, "He who hesitates is lost!" Achieving anything worthwhile demands diligent, consistent effort – not sporadic bursts of enthusiasm.

Jim Rohn's analogy is particularly apt:

> Some things you have to do every day. Eating seven apples on Saturday night instead of one a day just isn't going to get the job done.

The path ahead may seem daunting, but stay true to your dreams and persevere. If you refuse to give up, obstacles lose their power to stop you. Your ability to endure and continue taking one step at a time will eventually pay off. Consistency cannot be denied – it will deliver!

Slacking off or doing things in a sporadic manner causes a loss in momentum. Like riding a bicycle, you need to be moving to maintain your balance – you can't maintain your balance sitting still. Most people fail to achieve their goals due to inconsistent efforts. They expect quick, smooth progress, and when things don't go as planned, they become discouraged and decide to 'take a break' and return to it later. Taking a "break" will likely cause a loss in momentum and require backtracking or starting over from scratch.

Here is a perfect analogy that shows how the natural Law of Momentum operates.

The Airplane Analogy

Imagine you're sitting in the cockpit of a small airplane with the engines running and the nose pointed down the runway. You pull the throttle full, and the airplane races down the runway, gains speed, and takes off. You need to be at full throttle, and the plane will keep climbing. Once the airplane reaches a certain altitude, you pull the throttle back a little because you don't need the same amount of power to keep going. Besides, when you reach cruising altitude, you have to ease off a little, or you will burn out the engines.

Let's say you're in a plane zooming down the runway and decide to slow it down by pulling back on the throttle. What do you think the outcome would be?

The plane would fail to reach the necessary speed for takeoff and remain earthbound.

The Law of Momentum can also be described using the concept of escape velocity. Escape velocity is the speed at which an object, such as a rocket, can escape or break free from the gravity of a planet, moon, or other body without further propulsion. In other words, it must travel fast enough so that it will not fall back down. That speed is called the escape velocity.

To escape from the earth's gravity, a rocket has to travel at a speed greater than escape velocity. If the rocket doesn't have the power to accelerate to a speed faster than escape velocity, it will fall back to Earth without getting anywhere close to its target or destination. However, once it 'escapes,' the resistance decreases dramatically, and it's like the feeling of finally pulling your boot out of deep mud; suddenly, you're free!

The laws of the Universe are precise. When you embark on a new journey or project, you should go all in to create momentum. Don't slow down;

keep the momentum going until things are running smoothly, and only then can you ease off a bit.

Recognize that with major projects, there's always a 'drag' – something to slow you down. Like an airplane facing wind and gravity, you'll face unforeseen challenges. It is in these challenging moments that it becomes necessary to show resolve and pick up momentum despite the drag.

10.1.4 Apply Leverage

You grow in prosperity according to your associations. Like a chameleon, you take on the characteristics of your environment and tend to blend in.

An Enlightened Thought for Reflection

"It's better to hang out with people better than you. Pick out associates whose behavior is better than yours and you'll drift in that direction."

~ Warren Buffet

Psychologists suggest that as much as 90% of a person's success is determined by their reference group – the people they regularly associate with. Associate with positive, progressive individuals of high integrity and moral character. Seek out those with clear goals and plans, people progressing in life with lofty aspirations. As Zig Ziglar colorfully stated, *"You can't scratch with the turkeys if you want to fly with the eagles."*

Limit your association with toxic people. We are not referring to individuals who are unwell, but rather to those who are healthy and spend a lot of their time complaining and blaming others for their unfavorable situation instead of taking action to improve it.

Successful people use leverage extensively. They leverage other people's time, effort, money, knowledge, skills, contacts, credibility, systems, tools, and other resources. They pay for the opportunity to leverage because the benefits far outweigh the cost. This is a powerful concept!

They recognize that paying for leverage often yields benefits far outweighing the cost. This is a critical concept! You might pay someone $25 an hour to mow your lawn, freeing you to earn $100 in your area of expertise. Often, leveraging is the only way to achieve certain outcomes, as you may lack all the necessary skills or resources to accomplish everything alone.

When you assemble your team, you bring your dream to life. Take charge and embrace the role of leader or orchestrator. Most people shy away from leadership, fearing the responsibility and accountability it entails. Invariably, those willing to lead reap the greatest rewards. And the remarkable thing is that it's often easier.

Leadership isn't about doing everything yourself; it's about mobilizing others to work together toward a shared vision. Take charge like the conductor of an orchestra, blending talents into a harmonious whole. Your goal is to create a magnificent symphony with your life, to make it a breathtaking performance. The most effective way to achieve this is by leveraging others' resources.

Always seek win-win outcomes with those who assist you in achieving your goals. Maintain a sense of team spirit and shared purpose. Be a team player first and foremost. Recognize our interdependence – that's where true power lies. No one succeeds in isolation; the notion of a completely self-made individual is a myth. We all receive help in varying degrees.

Consider this remarkable illustration of shared effort, beautifully demonstrated by geese:

Lessons From Geese

When you see geese heading south for the winter, they fly in a V formation. Science has discovered why they fly that way. The following exposition is by Dr. Robert McNish (a former science teacher).

1. As each bird flaps its wings, it creates an uplift for the bird immediately behind. Flying in a V formation increases the flock's flying range by at least 71% compared to individual flight. (*People sharing a common direction and sense of community reach their destination more quickly and easily by traveling on each other's momentum.*)
2. When a goose falls out of formation, it suddenly feels the drag and resistance of flying alone. It quickly rejoins the formation to benefit from the lifting power of the bird in front. (*If we have as much sense as geese, we'll stay in formation with those headed where we want to go.*)
3. When the lead goose tires, it rotates back into the formation, and another goose flies point. (*It pays to take turns doing hard jobs. Like geese, people are interdependent on each other's skills, capabilities, and resources.*)
4. The geese honk from behind to encourage those up front to maintain their speed. (*We need to ensure our "honking" is encouraging. In groups where there is encouragement, production is much greater.*)
5. When a goose becomes sick or wounded and falls out, two other geese fall out of formation and follow it down to help and protect it. They stay with the fallen goose until it can fly again or dies. Only then do they launch out on their own or with another formation to catch up with their group. (*If we have the sense of a goose, we will stand by each other in times of need.*)

(Widemark, 2009)

Recognize that teamwork divides the task and multiplies the success!

Leverage is a simple yet compelling concept for achieving success in any endeavor. It's about working smarter, not just harder. Regardless of your profession, you can always magnify your results by applying the power of leverage.

10.2   Change Your Self-Talk...the Universe is Listening!

Self-talk refers to the ongoing inner conversation in your mind. It is the voice that comments on your life, choices, and emotions. This internal dialogue can either lift you or bring you down. It shapes how you feel, the energy you bring to your day, the quality of your relationships, and your performance in everything you do.

Your inner dialogue is more important than any other form of communication. You are both your toughest critic and your biggest supporter. Every minute you're awake, you converse with yourself using between 800 and 1,200 words. In these quiet moments, you either solve problems or create them, make decisions or avoid them, and either criticize, praise, or motivate yourself. You can focus on past mistakes or set the stage for a better future.

Psychologists suggest that if you were to record all your self-talk throughout the day, you'd likely find that much of it is negative and self-defeating. Without realizing it, the Law of Attraction is working in the background, meaning that when you focus on negative stuff, you may actually be drawing more negativity into your life. Negative self-talk can undermine your success and prevent you from reaching your full potential.

In the computer world, there's a phrase: GIGO – 'garbage in, garbage out.' This concept also applies to your mind. What you tell yourself influences how you live. When you focus on your limitations, they become your reality. This is the power of a self-fulfilling prophecy. Your subconscious mind takes your self-talk at face value. It doesn't question whether your words are true or false – it simply acts on them.

So, when you tell yourself, "It's too hard; I'm a failure; I'm always stuck," your subconscious responds, "It must be true," and it generates the energy to bring that outcome into your life. If negative self-talk continues, your subconscious will work to turn those negative thoughts into your reality. It's important to avoid negative self-talk.

Negative self-talk also impacts your physical health. It can increase stress, leading to high blood pressure, a weakened immune system, and even chronic diseases. On the other hand, positive self-talk can reduce stress, improve mental health, and contribute to overall wellness.

The first step in changing your self-talk is to become aware of your negative thoughts. Pay attention to what's going through your mind during the day. If you can, write them down. This simple act helps you become more conscious of your internal dialogue.

Once you've identified your negative thoughts, start questioning them. Ask yourself if they are really true. Often, we accept these thoughts as facts when they're just opinions or fears. Look for evidence that contradicts these negative beliefs. Consider other explanations or perspectives.

For example, if you catch yourself thinking, "I always mess things up," challenge that thought by asking, "Is that really true? Can I think of times when I've succeeded?" This process helps weaken the power of negative thinking.

Next, replace negative thoughts with positive, realistic ones. Instead of saying, "I can't do this," say, "I can succeed if I put in the effort and practice." Change your perspective by seeking new knowledge. Read books that inspire you. Participate in workshops. Surround yourself with positive people and immerse yourself in content that lifts you.

Positive actions lead to positive feelings, which in turn leads to positive self-talk. When you speak kindly to yourself, you create empowering images in your mind. These images inspire you to take the steps that lead to success.

What you say to yourself truly matters because it directly affects your energy and vibration, profoundly impacting your life. Change your inner dialogue, and you will improve your performance, feel more hopeful, and see better results.

The time it takes to see the effects of positive self-talk varies from person to person. Some people notice changes in their mindset and behavior within weeks, while for others, it may take several months. The key is to be consistent and patient. Over time, positive self-talk becomes second nature, leading to long-lasting improvements in your life.

Start today and experience the transformational power of positive self-talk.

10.3   Maintain Your Focus Without Wavering

You are the scriptwriter of your life, shaping every moment with your thoughts. You are the sum of your thoughts, as all thought is creative. To bring your desires into reality, you must keep your goals at the forefront of your mind and let them dominate your thinking.

The Law of Focus requires you to be *single-minded* in pursuing your outcomes. Concentrate all your attention to what you want and fuel it with emotion. If you constantly dwell on what you don't want, you'll manifest it. As the saying goes, "*What you resist, persists.*"

A timeless parable from the *Mahabharata* illustrates the importance of focus:

The Power of Focus

Arjuna, the third son of Queen Kunti, was an archer known for his passion and dedication. He practiced tirelessly, becoming the finest archer in his land. His teacher, Gurudev, favored him, which made his two older brothers jealous.

One day, the brothers openly accused Gurudev of being biased. To settle the matter, Gurudev set up a test to find the best archer. He placed a wooden bird on a distant tree, partly concealed by branches. The challenge was to shoot an arrow through the bird's eye.

Gurudev first invited the eldest son to shoot. Before he released his arrow, Gurudev asked, "O eldest son of Queen Kunti, what do you see?"

The eldest son replied, "I see you, the tree, the bird, and the people around us."

"Shoot," said Gurudev.

The eldest son took aim but missed.

Next, Gurudev called the second son to demonstrate his skill. Before he released his arrow, Gurudev asked, "O second son of Queen Kunti, what do you see?"

Anticipating a more targeted answer, he quickly replied, "I see the tree and the bird."

"Shoot," Gurudev instructed. He, too, missed.

Then it was Arjuna's turn. Gurudev asked, "O Arjuna, what do you see?"

"I see only the eye of the bird," Arjuna replied.

"Do you see the tree, the bird, or the people around you?" Gurudev asked.

"No," Arjuna responded. "I see only the bird's eye."

"Shoot," said Gurudev. Arjuna let his arrow fly, hitting the bird right in the eye.

"Well done," said Gurudev. He explained to the others that Arjuna's success was due to his intense focus, which gave him the advantage. It was his singular concentration that made him the best student.

~ Mahabharata

The lesson is clear: envision the outcome you want and hold that image in your mind. Do not let distractions pull you away from your goal. Like Arjuna, focus on the task at hand with undivided attention.

An Enlightened Thought for Reflection

"Concentrate all your thoughts upon the work at hand. The sun's rays do not burn until brought to a focus."

~ Alexander Graham Bell

Just as the sun's rays, when concentrated through a magnifying glass, can start a fire, your attention, when focused on key activities, allows you to perform at an extraordinary level. But, if you scatter your energy like the sun, you will warm everything and have little impact on anything. To have a significant impact, focus your energy on what you truly want.

A laser beam is another perfect example of the power of focused energy. A laser's highly concentrated light can cut through steel, whereas dispersed light cannot. Likewise, if your energy is scattered across many areas, your results will be weak. But when you focus on one task with intensity, you create a "laser beam" of power, achieving specific and impactful results.

More than a century ago, Swami Vivekananda emphasized the same idea:

> Take up one idea. Make that idea your life; think of it, dream of it, live on that idea. Let the brain, the muscles, the nerves, every part of your body be full of that idea. This is the way to success.

You might ask: how can the muscles, the nerves, and every part of your body be full of an idea? It's because of your subconscious mind! It's a goal-achieving mechanism comprising every cell in your body – your entire being! Therefore, when you focus single-mindedly on a goal, your whole body resonates, hums, and pulsates with your desired outcome!

The Power of Commitment

Success isn't about age, gender, education, or background. History and modern times are full of people from all walks of life who have defied the odds to achieve greatness. As Scottish writer Thomas Carlyle put it:

> The weakest living creature, by concentrating his powers on a single object, can accomplish something; whereas the strongest, by dispersing his over many, may fail to accomplish anything.

Similarly, American minister Harry Emerson Fosdick observed:

> No steam or gas drives anything until it is confined. No Niagara is ever turned into light and power until it is tunneled. No life ever grows great until it is focused, dedicated, and disciplined.

Top athletes, like world-class tennis players, know the value of focus. Their mind isn't drifting off to other things. They stay completely engaged in the moment, knowing that every shot counts. They are so focused that they literally cannot take their eyes off the ball. Their ability to focus intensely can be the conclusive factor in winning a championship. In the same way, you are world-class material, too!

Visualization: A Powerful Tool

Visualization is a proven technique for staying focused. Many athletes use it to mentally practice their performance before a competition. This process helps maintain focus, boosts confidence, and prepares them for the real event.

When you hold a clear image of your goal in your mind, you're more likely to stay committed and driven, even when distractions threaten to pull you off course. But visualization alone won't carry you across the finish line – it demands commitment. Visualization plants the seed, but commitment is what nurtures it into reality.

Commitment is a critical ingredient in any recipe for success. To commit is to dedicate yourself fully to a goal. When you're truly committed to an outcome, it happens, no matter what – come "hell or high water." Commitment drives action. Without it, nothing gets accomplished.

There's a big difference between being interested in something and being committed to it. When you're merely interested, you'll pursue it only when convenient. But when you're truly committed, you'll do whatever it takes, no excuses.

As Wolfgang von Goethe said:

> Until one is committed there is always hesitancy, the chance to draw back, always ineffectiveness. Concerning all acts of initiative (and creation), there is one elementary truth, the ignorance of which kills countless ideas and splendid plans: that the moment one definitively commits oneself, then Providence moves too. All sorts of things occur to help one that would never otherwise have occurred. A whole stream of events issues from the decision, raising in one's favor all manner of

unforeseen incidents and meetings and material assistance, which no man could have dreamt would have come his way.

Once you commit, unexpected support shows up. Things fall into place in ways you never imagined.

Stick to the Basics

To succeed, focus all your energy on your current project and commit to seeing it through. Achieving long-lasting success requires a consistent, laser-like focus. Establish daily habits that support this, such as setting specific goals, working in a distraction-free environment, using time management techniques, and practicing mindfulness or meditation.

Keep your eyes on the prize and be patient with yourself. Maintaining focus requires effort, but the benefits are well worth it. With consistent focus, you'll accomplish extraordinary things and realize your full potential.

10.4   Don't Broadcast Your Goals and Successes

Be cautious about whom you share your goals and achievements with. Take care not to attract unnecessary attention. While it may be difficult to accept, some people would rather see you fail than succeed. Unfortunately, this is human nature. Those who are not actively working to improve their own lives often take satisfaction in the setbacks of others. They might even enjoy gossiping about someone's misfortune. If you reflect on this, you'll likely agree that it's true.

Every dream you share can cause jealousy, a negative emotion often directed towards you. Pursuing your dreams takes courage, which says a lot about your character. Many people envy this kind of bravery. Rather than applauding it, they may try to bring you down to their level, as shown in this story:

The Crab Bucket

A man walking along the beach came across a fisherman with a bucket of crabs beside him. Noticing the bucket wasn't covered, the man asked the fisherman why he didn't secure the crabs to stop them from escaping. The fisherman explained, "Crabs have a 'mass mentality.' If there's only one crab in the bucket, it will quickly climb out. But when there are many crabs, if one tries to climb up, the others grab it and pull it back down so that it shares their fate."

This behavior is not exclusive to crabs; humans do the same thing. When someone tries to better themselves, chase a dream, or change their circumstances, others may try to pull them back down. Whether it's out of jealousy, fear, or a desire to maintain the status quo, people resist change, especially if it makes them question their own choices.

Even those closest to you, such as family and friends, may unintentionally discourage your growth. They might not mean harm, but they'll list reasons why your dreams won't come true. They might even mock you for aiming high or, worse, for failing. Sometimes, the people who are supposed to support you the most are the ones who question your plans or suggest that they are unrealistic.

Your dreams are precious, and negativity from others can influence them. That's why it's essential to protect your ideas and aspirations from those who don't appreciate them. By keeping your goals and successes to yourself, you can shield them from jealousy and pessimism. After all, you have a unique purpose, and pursuing your highest potential can make a difference in the world.

Choose Your Support Wisely

Share your ambitions only with those who genuinely support you and compliment your progress. There's nothing more discouraging than revealing a goal you care about to someone only to have them dismiss it as unrealistic or unworthy. Those who truly stand by you will share your excitement, encouraging you to push past obstacles. They will be there for you in both your struggles and your successes.

As you bring your dreams to life, be careful not to boast or show off. Be careful not to present your achievements in a self-centered way. Bragging shifts the energy you give off and can attract resentment and jealousy. Let your accomplishments speak for themselves, and when it's appropriate to share them, do so with humility. Humility nurtures respect and creates positive energy around you.

Celebrate Your Success with Gratitude

When you achieve success, don't forget the people who helped you along the way. Acknowledge and thank them, whether their contributions were big or small. Show your appreciation for their support. Also, share the knowledge and strategies you've gained from your experiences. By doing so, you not only enjoy your own success but also help others on their journey to achieving theirs.

Success is more rewarding when shared with those who support you, and when you help others achieve their full potential.

10.5   Ready, Fire, Aim – The Power of Swift Execution

Success loves speed. In our fast-changing world, the key to achieving your dreams lies not just in what you know, but in how quickly you put that knowledge into action. Speed of execution is about taking action on your best ideas and strategies as quickly as possible and then moving on to the next opportunity without hesitation.

Everyone has good intentions, but intentions alone don't make things happen. It's the execution that distinguishes those who make a difference from those who simply drift through life. Consider this: How many great ideas have you had that never came to fruition? How many opportunities have slipped through your fingers because you were stuck in the planning phase, waiting for the perfect moment? It's time to break that cycle and adopt a new approach to success.

The mantra for extraordinary achievement isn't "Ready, Aim, Fire." It's "Ready, Fire, Aim." This might sound counterintuitive, but it's a turning point. Here's why:

1. Action Breeds Learning: When you take action, even if you miss your target, you gain invaluable firsthand experience. You learn what works and what doesn't in real-time.

2. Failure is Your Friend: Don't just accept failure – welcome it with open arms! Each misstep is a stepping stone to success. The most accomplished individuals often have a longer list of failures than successes. It's part of the journey.

3. Speed Trumps Perfection: In today's busy world, it's not the big that eat the small; it's the fast that beat the slow. The ability to execute quickly gives you a significant edge over those who are still perfecting their plans.

Embrace the Power of Swift Action

Imagine you're learning to ride a bicycle. You can spend hours studying the physics of balance, the optimal posture, and the perfect pedaling technique. But until you actually get on that bike and start pedaling, you won't truly learn how to ride. You might fall a few times, but each tumble teaches you something new. Before you know it, you're cruising down the street, the wind in your hair, experiencing the thrill of success.

This principle applies to every aspect of life. The most successful people minimize the gap between learning and doing. They don't wait for perfect conditions or absolute certainty. They act, learn, adjust, and act again. It's not about perfection; it's about momentum.

In education, there's a phenomenon called The Matthew Effect: children who learn to read early read more, becoming even better readers, creating a widening gap between them and their peers over time. The same principle holds true in both life and business. Those who act quickly gain experience faster, learn more, and therefore achieve more.

Develop a Sense of Urgency

Approach everything with a sense of urgency. Only a small percentage of people have a true bias for action; these are the movers and shakers of the world – the people who get results. When you develop a strong sense of urgency and importance for your goals, you set yourself apart from the crowd, positioning yourself in the top tier of your field.

Joseph Cyril Bamford, the visionary founder of JCB Manufacturing, once said:

> *No matter how intelligent or capable you may be, if you lack a sense of urgency, now is the time to develop it. The world is full of competent people who intend to do things tomorrow or "when they get around to it." However, their accomplishments rarely match those of less talented individuals blessed with a sense of urgency and a determination to act now.*

Don't get caught in the trap of endless deliberation. If an idea shows promise, don't wait until you've ironed out every detail. Create a basic plan and get moving. You'll learn more in the first week of action than in a month of planning.

Ponder the wisdom of Napoleon Hill, esteemed author of the timeless classic "Think and Grow Rich":

Create a definite plan for carrying out your desire and begin at once, whether you are ready or not, to put this plan into action.

Successful people don't wait for the perfect moment. They don't wait for all the traffic lights to turn green before beginning their journey. They act regardless of their circumstance. In contrast, unsuccessful people rarely implement what they learn. They spend too much time overthinking and planning without ever taking action.

Learn Through Action

Every action you take, successful or not, is a learning opportunity. Even when things don't go as planned, you gain valuable insights. You figure out what doesn't work, which is just as important as knowing what does. The real world provides the most accurate feedback, allowing you to fine-tune your approach.

If your first attempt doesn't yield the desired results, don't be discouraged. Change your strategy and try again. The goal is to fail forward, turning each mistake into a stepping stone towards your ultimate success.

Don't be tempted to make excuses for not starting. Don't talk your way to success – act your way there. The best time to act is always now.

Accept this simple formula:

1. The faster you act, the more you achieve.
2. The more you achieve, the more experience you gain.
3. The more experience you gain, the more competent you become.
4. The more competent you become, the better your results.
5. The better your results, the greater your rewards in life.

It really is that straightforward!

Let the profound words of Dr. Benjamin E. Mays inspire you to make the most of every moment:

You only have a minute,
Only 60 seconds in it,
Forced upon you, can't refuse it,
Didn't seek it, didn't choose it.
You must suffer if you lose it,
Give account if you abuse it.
It's just a tiny little minute,
But your whole future is in it.

Your future is shaped by the actions you take right now. Each minute is a gift packed with potential. Don't let it slip away. Seize it, use it, and watch as your swift actions turn your dreams into reality.

Remember, in the game of life, it's not always the strongest or the smartest who wins. More often than not, it's those who are quickest to act, most willing to learn from their mistakes, and most persistent in pursuing their goals.

The time is now. Ready, fire, aim – and watch your life transform in amazing ways!

10.6   Make Sacrifices and Practice Self-Discipline

Success doesn't come from luck or talent alone. It often requires giving up something valuable in the short term to achieve something more significant in the long term. This is where sacrifice comes in. Whether it's time, comfort, or even relationships, letting go of something valuable is often necessary on the road to success.

Economists have a term for this: opportunity cost. It's the value of what you give up when you make a choice. When you choose to study instead of watching your favorite show, the opportunity cost is the enjoyment you would have had from that show. The Oxford Dictionary describes this idea perfectly, defining sacrifice as "the act of giving up something valued for the sake of something more important or worthy."

Short-term Sacrifices for Long-term Rewards

The sacrifices you make today are the foundation of your future achievements. They're investments in yourself that can yield incredible returns, whether that's financial security, career progress, or personal growth.

Successful people understand this principle deeply. They're willing to forego immediate pleasures – like leisure time, or inconsequential spending – to focus on their goals. They ask themselves, "What am I willing to give up to achieve the results I desire?" And then they act on their answers.

This willingness to sacrifice is what sets achievers apart. They recognize that in the beginning, there's often an imbalance. You might pour in effort, time, and resources without seeing immediate rewards. It might feel like "all work and no pay" for a while. Regardless, they persist because they understand that this imbalance is temporary and necessary for long-term success.

Many understand this principle intellectually, but few apply it consistently. This lack of discipline is why many fall short of their potential. If you're always seeking instant gratification, lasting success will remain elusive.

Discipline and Sacrifice: A Powerful Partnership

Discipline and sacrifice are inseparable. Discipline gives you the strength to make sacrifices, and those sacrifices, in turn, reinforce your discipline. This creates a positive cycle that propels you toward your goals.

Life is full of distractions that can derail your progress. To succeed, you must remain focused on your goal and persevere until you reach it. Discipline isn't a trait you're born with – it's a skill you can develop through conscious effort. It's about training yourself to take the right actions, at the right time, in the right way.

Human nature often pushes us to seek the path of least resistance, to expend as little energy as possible. But success doesn't come by chance or by taking shortcuts. It comes through consistent, focused effort. Because most people are looking for an easy way out, if you cultivate the discipline to do what's necessary, you'll face little competition. Your success becomes almost inevitable.

An Enlightened Thought for Reflection

The heights by great men reached and kept
Were not attained by sudden flight,
But they, while their companions slept,
Were toiling upward in the night.

~ Henry Wadsworth Longfellow

In 1940, Albert E. N. Gray, an insurance industry official, delivered a speech that revealed what he called the common denominator of success – the one quality shared by all successful people. He stated that *"successful people form the habit of doing the things that failures don't like to do."*

Gray elaborated: *"The things that failures don't like to do are the very same things you and I – and even highly successful people – don't like to do. The reality is that success is achieved by a minority, and therefore, it's not something attained by following our natural preferences or dislikes."*

He emphasized that successful people accomplish their goals by doing what's necessary, even when it's not enjoyable. Failures, on the other hand, focus on seeking comfort. Successful people are driven by the desire for *pleasing results,* whereas failures are motivated by *pleasing methods,* settling for whatever results come easily.

The good news is that habits are learned, which means they can also be unlearned and replaced. You have the power to change your habits and develop the discipline you need to succeed.

An Enlightened Thought for Reflection

It is one of the strange ironies of this strange life that those who work the hardest, who subject themselves to the strictest discipline, who give up certain pleasurable things in order to achieve a goal, are the happiest.

~ Brutus Hamilton

Sacrifice and Discipline as the Foundations of Success

Sacrifice and discipline are essential building blocks for success. When you choose your actions, you also choose the consequences. You can "pay now and play later" or "play now and pay later." The choice is yours. Now is the time to make sacrifices so you can reap the rewards later in life.

Motivational speaker Jim Rohn wisely noted that life presents two types of pain: the pain of discipline and the pain of regret. He explained that the pain of discipline weighs ounces, while the pain of regret weighs tons. The message is clear: the pain of regret is far more difficult to bear than the effort required for discipline.

Accept the challenge. Develop the discipline to make sacrifices and the willpower to stay the course. The rewards will come and be worth every bit of effort you've invested. Your future self will thank you for the sacrifices you make today. So, take that first step, make that first sacrifice, and watch as it sets you on the path to extraordinary success.

10.7   Take Risks and Fail Forward – It's the Safest Way to Go!

Imagine a world where failure isn't a dirty word but a stepping stone to greatness. Welcome to the true path to success! In this world, failure isn't something to fear; it's something to embrace, learn from, and use as fuel for your journey to the top.

Let's start with a powerful truth from Dorothea Brande:

Act boldly, and unseen forces will come to your aid.

This isn't just a nice quote – it's a call to action. It's an invitation to be courageous, to take risks, and to trust that the universe has your back. Your willingness to step out of your comfort zone is evidence of your faith in something greater than yourself. To achieve all that is possible, dare to attempt the seemingly impossible. Take advantage of opportunities when they present themselves and, at the same time, minimize failure or loss by intelligently assessing potential risks and rewards. This balance of boldness and wisdom is what sets the truly successful apart.

Success: A Numbers Game You Can Win

Success isn't just about talent – it's about persistence. The more you try, the more likely you are to succeed. Highly successful people have tried (and failed) far more than the average person. By the law of probability, the more opportunities you pursue, the higher your chances of finding the one that works for you.

Your attitude toward risk-taking is one of the most important indicators of your readiness for success. Every person who's ever done something remarkable has had to leave the safety of the shore and sail into uncharted waters. Growth and learning always happen outside your comfort zone. Yes, it's scary out there, but you know what's scarier? Staying put and watching life pass you by.

An Enlightened Thought for Reflection

There are risks and costs to any program of action, but they are far less than the long-range risks and costs of comfortable inaction.

~ John F. Kennedy

If you're content with being average, stick to the well-worn path. But if you're aiming for the stars, you need to blaze your own trail. Those in the top 1% are constantly pushing boundaries and taking risks. Every day, ask yourself: *"Am I doing what the other 99% aren't?"* If you're not, you're likely part of the 99%. Taking risks sets you apart from the crowd.

An Enlightened Thought for Reflection

Progress always involves risk. You can't steal second base and keep your foot on first.

~ *Frederick B. Wilcox*

The Law of Opposites: Embracing the Duality of Success

Life operates on the principle of balance. Just as there's no light without darkness, no up without down, there's no reward without risk. This isn't just philosophy – it's a practical truth that affects to every aspect of your life:

- Want to make money? You've got to risk losing some.
- Craving deep, meaningful relationships? You need to risk being vulnerable.
- Aiming to be a top athlete? You must risk injury.
- Dreaming big? You have to risk falling short.

But here's the million-dollar question: Are these really risks, or are they simply the price of admission for an extraordinary life?

An Enlightened Thought for Reflection

Far better to dare mighty things, to win glorious triumphs, even though checkered by failure, than to take rank with those poor spirits who neither enjoy much nor suffer much, because they live in the gray twilight that knows not victory, nor defeat.

~ *Theodore Roosevelt*

Living itself is a risk. But it's a risk worth taking, as beautifully captured in the following poem by Janet Rand:

Risks

To laugh is to risk appearing the fool.
To weep is to risk being called sentimental.
To reach out to another is to risk involvement.
To expose feelings is to risk showing your true self.
To place your ideas and your dreams before the crowd is
to risk being called naive.
To love is to risk not being loved in return.
To live is to risk dying.
To hope is to risk despair.
To try is to risk failure.

But risks must be taken because the greatest risk in life is to risk nothing. The person who risks nothing, does nothing, has nothing, is nothing, and becomes nothing. He may avoid suffering and sorrow, but he simply cannot learn, feel, change, grow, or love. Chained by his certitude, he is a slave; he has forfeited his freedom. Only the person who risks is truly free.

~ Janet Rand

The Power of Calculated Risks

Now, let's be clear: we're not talking about reckless abandon here. We're talking about calculated risks – bold moves made with careful consideration. It's about stepping out on that limb, but first making sure it can hold your weight.

Successful people aren't gamblers throwing caution to the wind. They're strategic risk-takers, evaluating each opportunity, weighing the potential outcomes, and then making informed decisions. They understand that reasonable, responsible risk-taking is the vehicle that guides them towards their goals.

Remember Thomas Edison – the lightbulb guy? He famously said, *"I have not failed. I've just found 10,000 ways that won't work."* Each of those 10,000 attempts was a calculated risk. Each "failure" was a lesson learned, bringing him one step closer to inventing the light bulb. Edison's story isn't about never failing – it's about never giving up.

Learning from Failure: Your Secret Weapon

Every failure is a goldmine of information about yourself. It reveals your values, tests your determination, and shows how badly you want to succeed. By examining your failures, you gain insights that help you make better decisions and avoid repeating mistakes.

Embrace these lessons – they make you stronger, smarter, and more resilient. They are the key elements that turn an ordinary person into an extraordinary success story.

Life is all about growth and blossoming into the best version of yourself. And growth only happens when you push past your current limits and dare to do what you haven't mastered yet.

An Enlightened Thought for Reflection

And the day came when the risk it took to remain tight inside the bud was more painful than the risk it took to blossom.

~ Anais Nin

The British Special Air Service has a motto that sums it up perfectly: *"Who dares, wins!"* It's time for you to dare. It's time for you to win. Whenever you take a risk, you give yourself the chance to soar. The sky's the limit – but only if you're brave enough to spread your wings and fly.

10.8 Deal with the Crisis – Innovate, Differentiate, Accelerate

Life is a never-ending education, filled with experiences that challenge and shape us. Some of these experiences will push us to our limits, forcing us to grow in ways we never imagined. Others may feel like insurmountable obstacles, transforming into full-blown crises. But here's the hidden gem: every crisis, no matter how daunting, carries within it the seeds of opportunity.

Consider this: Hardship and struggle aren't reserved for the unfortunate few – they're universal experiences that affect us all. And often, it's the situations we'd never choose for ourselves that teach us the most valuable lessons.

It's through these hard times that we prepare for greater accomplishments. The human spirit shines brightest when it overcomes adversity, revealing strengths we never knew we possessed.

Soichiro Honda is a shining example of how to innovate, differentiate, and accelerate progress in the face of adversity. He turned multiple crises into successes, ultimately building one of the most recognizable brands in the world – the Honda Motor Company.

The Remarkable Soichiro Honda

Picture Japan in the 1930s, a nation grappling with the Great Depression. In the midst of this economic turmoil, we find Soichiro Honda, an expert auto mechanic, with his own workshop in Hamamatsu. In 1938, fueled by ambition and a dream, Honda started a small factory to manufacture piston rings for motor car engines.

His goal? To sell these piston rings to Toyota. Honda poured his heart and soul into this venture, working tirelessly day and night. He even slept in his workshop, driven by an unshakable belief that he could perfect his design and create a top-quality product. When funds ran low, he made the difficult decision to pawn his wife's jewelry to keep his business afloat.

Finally, after countless hours of work, Honda completed his piston ring. With high hopes, he presented his creation to Toyota – only to face bitter disappointment. Toyota rejected his product, claiming it didn't meet their standards. Adding insult to injury, Honda endured ridicule from engineers who laughed at his design.

But did Honda give up? Absolutely not. Instead of wallowing in failure, he chose to see it as a stepping stone to success. He went back to school, immersing himself in the study of metallurgy to gain a deeper understanding of how to work with metal. After two more years of relentless struggle and a complete redesign of his product, Honda's perseverance paid off. In 1940, he finally secured a contract with Toyota.

However, just as things were looking up, the world plunged into war. The Japanese government's war efforts led to a shortage of building materials, threatening Honda's ability to construct the factory he needed to fulfill his contract with Toyota. But Honda wasn't about to let this obstacle stop him. In a stroke of ingenuity, he invented a new concrete-making process that allowed him to build his factory despite the scarcity of materials.

With the factory built, Honda was ready to begin production. But fate had other plans. The factory was bombed twice, and steel became unavailable. Many would have seen this as the end of the road, but not Honda. He saw opportunity where others saw defeat. He began collecting surplus gasoline cans discarded by US fighters, jokingly calling them "Gifts from President Truman." These discarded cans became the raw material for his rebuilt manufacturing process.

Just when it seemed things couldn't get worse, an earthquake struck, destroying the factory. But even this catastrophe couldn't break Honda's spirit.

In the aftermath of the war, Japan faced an extreme gasoline shortage, forcing people to walk or use bicycles. For Honda, the daily bicycle ride to work was too slow. So, what did he do? He built a tiny engine and attached it to his bicycle. His neighbors, impressed by his innovation, wanted engines of their own. But once again, Honda faced a shortage of raw materials to build these engines.

Undeterred, Honda wrote to 18,000 bicycle store owners, penning an inspiring letter asking for their help in revitalizing Japan. Approximately 5,000 responded, supporting his quest to build small bicycle engines. The first models were bulky and impractical, but Honda didn't give up. He continued to develop and refine his design until he created "The Super Cub," a small engine that became an outstanding success. Not content with dominating the Japanese market, Honda began exporting his Super Cub motorcycles to Europe and America.

But the story doesn't end there. In the 1970s, another gas shortage hit, shifting automotive trends towards small cars. Honda, with his expertise in small engine design, was quick to capitalize on this trend. His company began producing compact cars, smaller than anything the market had seen before, riding another wave of success.

Today, the Honda Corporation stands as one of the world's largest automobile companies. This phenomenal success story stems from one man's steadfast commitment, his willingness to take action, and his ability to adapt continuously. For Soichiro Honda, failure was simply not an option.

Life's Lessons in Disguise

Honda's story isn't just a tale of business success; it's a powerful lesson in resilience and adaptability. Each setback he faced was an opportunity in disguise, orchestrated by the universe to test his commitment and his ability to innovate new solutions, differentiate himself in the marketplace, and accelerate the growth of his enterprises.

When pursuing ambitious goals, expect the universe to challenge your resolve. It's almost as if, just when everything seems perfect, a wrench gets thrown into the works. These moments aren't meant to derail you; they're invitations to focus more intently and find creative solutions.

It's easy to thrive when everything's going smoothly. But it's the trying times that reveal our true character, distinguishing those who merely talk from those who walk the talk.

As Epictetus wisely noted:

Circumstances do not make the man; they merely reveal him to himself.

Life's Grand Drama

Life is a series of events, each one an act in your personal drama. From the moment you wake up to the time you go to bed, you're participating in a continuous stream of experiences. Some of these events will be favorable, others not so much. What's interesting is that an event you perceive as unfavorable might be seen as favorable by someone else, and vice versa.

Regardless of how you perceive each event, your role is to actively participate in this spectacular drama of human existence. Make the best of each moment, whether it seems good or bad at first glance.

Some events in life are entirely within your control – like how you respond to an insult or what time to get out of bed. Other events, like the weather or the cycle of life and death, are completely beyond your control.

It's how you deal with these uncontrollable events that truly matter. While you can't change the event itself, you always have the power to choose your response. During challenging times, it's worth reflecting on the well-known words of theologian Reinhold Niebuhr:

God, grant me the serenity
To accept the things I cannot change;
Courage to change the things I can;
And wisdom to know the difference.

Focus your energy on the things you can influence. When faced with a challenging situation, consider Dale Carnegie's pragmatic advice:

First, ask yourself: What is the worst thing that can happen?
Then prepare to accept it.
Then proceed to improve on the worst.

The idea is to make the best of a bad situation calmly and collectedly rather than letting fear of the worst-case scenario paralyze you. Your ability to find opportunity in adversity is crucial to your success. Understand that while you may not control the situation, you always control your response to it.

The Flexibility Factor

One of the most defining characteristics of highly successful people is their ability to deal with crises and overcome adversity. They face challenges with remarkable flexibility, bending without breaking.

As Chin-Ning Chu beautifully illustrates:

The grass bends easily in the wind; the great oak stands unmoved. A strong wind can uproot the oak, but no wind, however strong, can uproot the grass that bends flat before it.

Bestselling author Brian Tracy observes that highly successful individuals seem to possess an inner switch they can flip when crisis strikes. Instead of reacting with frustration or panic, they become calm, focused, and deliberate. They take control of their emotions, gather information, and respond thoughtfully. They don't rush; they ask questions, stay polite, and show respect – saying "please" and "thank you" even in stressful moments.

Your Innate Resilience

Like any successful person, you, too, have an innate capacity for bouncing back. Rather than living in fear of the next crisis, prepare for life's storms with courage and enthusiasm. If life hands you a lemon, don't just make lemonade – open a lemonade stand! Accept life's ups and downs; let them strengthen you, and enjoy the calm that follows each storm.

Every crisis is an opportunity in disguise. It's a chance to grow, to learn, and to discover strengths you never knew you had. So, the next time you face a challenge, don't ask, "Why me?" Instead, ask, "What can I learn from this?" That tiny shift in perspective can reveal strengths you didn't even know you had. Sometimes, the hardest moments are just the universe's way of nudging you toward your next big breakthrough.

10.9   Do Whatever It Takes – 'Go the Whole Nine Yards'

When you set a goal, you're not just making a simple decision. You're entering into a powerful, unspoken agreement with the Universe. This contract has one essential clause: your willingness to do *whatever it takes* to achieve your desired outcome.

Imagine you're aiming to land your dream job or attract that special someone into your life. Are you ready to make any necessary sacrifice? Would you move across the country or even relocate abroad *if that's what it took*? You can't cherry-pick which steps you're willing to take and still expect to reach your goal. The Universe doesn't work that way.

While you always have the right to make personal choices, altering your commitment (like excluding a specific step) is akin to breaking your agreement with the Universe. You forfeit your right to the outcome you desire. Doing whatever it takes means exactly that – doing everything necessary to achieve your goal.

A powerful phrase captures this all-in mentality: "Go the whole nine yards." It originates from World War II fighter pilots, whose machine gun ammunition belts were 27 feet long – nine yards. When pilots fired every bullet, they had truly gone "the whole nine yards." It was a matter of life and death, a total commitment to their mission.

Now, ask yourself: Are you willing to go the whole nine yards for your goals? If not, you're not fully committed to your outcome. But when you show that determined willingness to do whatever is necessary, you send a clear signal to the Universe that you're dead serious about your ambitions.

Here's the interesting part: this willingness doesn't always mean you'll have to follow through on every challenging step. Often, simply being open to the possibility is enough. The Universe may not require you to endure every hardship. The key is your readiness. The Universe rewards that openness and flexibility.

Success comes at a cost. The Universe sets the price for your goal, and you must be willing to pay it in full. Every thought, word, and action toward your goal carries value. Sometimes, just demonstrating your willingness to tackle a challenge is enough for the Universe to grant you credit without making you actually do it. The Universe is compassionate and committed to guiding you toward your best path.

But don't think you can pull a fast one on the Universe. It knows your every thought, word, and deed. It will test your resolve. To help you attain the level of consciousness required to manifest your desires, the Universe will present you with various challenges and learning opportunities. When these moments arise, you've got to lean in, even if it means risking failure, enduring discomfort, or facing hardship. Growth doesn't exactly happen in cozy, cushioned places. Sometimes, it's about taking a deep breath and diving into the chaos. Only then will you prove that you're truly ready for your desired outcome.

Let's look at a real-life example of what it means to do whatever it takes. Chuck Yeager's historic achievement of breaking the sound barrier is a perfect illustration of this principle in action.

Breaking the Sound Barrier: Chuck Yeager's Story

Before Yeager's successful flight on October 14, 1947, no one had ever flown faster than the speed of sound. In fact, a previous attempt by a British pilot had ended in tragedy, underscoring the immense risks of supersonic flight.

Despite these dangers, the U.S. Air Force pushed forward with the development of the experimental Bell X-1 aircraft, explicitly designed to break the sound barrier. They needed a pilot brave enough to take on this mission, and they found that courage in Chuck Yeager. Many engineers feared the X-1 would disintegrate upon reaching supersonic speeds, but Yeager believed the intense vibrations would subside once the aircraft surpassed the sound barrier.

Fate, however, seemed determined to throw obstacles in Yeager's path. Just days before the flight, he fell off a horse and broke two ribs – an injury that could have easily disqualified him from the mission. But Yeager wasn't ready to give up. He taped up his ribs and kept quiet about his condition, determined to push forward.

On the day of the flight, another problem arose – his injured ribs made it impossible for him to shut the door of the Bell X-1. Yeager confided in Jack Ridley, the flight engineer, who ingeniously fashioned a makeshift lever from a broomstick handle so Yeager could close the hatch using his left hand.

Once in the air, Yeager faced violent vibrations that threatened to tear the aircraft apart. But he pushed on, trusting his belief that things would smooth out once the aircraft reached Mach 1. Sure enough, at Mach 0.96, the vibrations stopped, and the Bell X-1 broke through the sound barrier.

This singular feat shattered not only the sound barrier but also the prevailing doubts and limitations that had held back aviation progress. The thunderous sonic boom that echoed across the desert wasn't just the sound of breaking the sound barrier; it was the roar of human ingenuity and determination. Yeager's triumph is a powerful reminder that even the most ambitious goals can be achieved through courage, perseverance, and a willingness to face the unknown.

Yeager's story holds valuable lessons for all of us. Based on our understanding of the Universe and its laws, we could argue that his horse-riding accident was no coincidence. When you ask for a significant outcome, the Universe often tests your readiness. It may pull the rug out from under you, forcing you to reconsider your actions and commitment.

In Yeager's case, falling off that horse and breaking his ribs might have seemed like a clear signal to abandon his mission. But Yeager was tough and determined, willing to take a calculated risk. He believed that once he was in the pilot's seat, he could handle the flight. He was ready to do his part, and the Universe aligned events to support him.

Breaking the sound barrier was one of many incredible achievements in Yeager's service to his country. Little did he know, he had spent years preparing for this moment. It is reported that when he wasn't flying, he studied every aspect of every plane, down to the smallest detail. Such was his passion for aviation! By pushing his limits, challenging conventions, and doing whatever it took in his career, Yeager had grown in consciousness and become the person he needed to *be* to achieve greatness.

The Qur'an offers a powerful insight that resonates with Yeager's journey:

> *Do you think that you shall enter the Garden of Bliss without such trials as came to those who passed before you?*

This timeless wisdom reminds us that challenges aren't merely hurdles in the way – they're like the chisels that carve us into something greater. Those trials, though exhausting and sometimes maddening, don't just test us; they prepare us to carry the weight of the success we seek.

There are no shortcuts to success. If you're not willing to "go the whole nine yards," perhaps it's time to reconsider your goal. Find one that sets your heart on fire, something you are willing to pursue till completion relentlessly.

All the same, realize that relentless pursuit is about more than external accomplishments; it's also about maintaining balance in all other essential aspects of your life. A balanced lifestyle supports the energy, focus, and resilience you need to chase your dreams.

Remember the age-old wisdom:

> *Where there's a will, there's a way.*

This simple phrase captures the essence of doing whatever it takes. When your will is strong enough, you'll find a way to overcome any obstacle, navigate any challenge, and achieve your goals.

Go forth, embrace the challenges, welcome the tests, and be willing to do whatever it takes. The Universe is ready to support you every step of the way.

10.10   Never, Never, Never Give Up

Chasing your goals isn't just about reaching the finish line; it's a wild ride packed with life lessons you didn't even know you needed, moments of raw growth, and startling flashes of self-discovery that hit you when you least expect them. And the secret to tapping into all this transformative power is deceptively simple: *never give up*.

Many people fall short of their dreams not because they lack talent or opportunity, but because they quit too soon. They let obstacles become roadblocks instead of stepping stones. But you're different. You'll be the one who perseveres, pushes through, and refuses to let setbacks define your story.

There will always be challenges. They're part of the journey. Resolve in advance that no matter what setbacks you face, you will never give up. Make a commitment to yourself to keep moving forward – not just when it's easy, but especially when it's hard.

When you hit a roadblock (and you will), take a deep breath. Step back. Look at the big picture. Break the problem down into smaller, more manageable pieces. Tackle each piece one by one. Suddenly, that insurmountable obstacle becomes a series of challenges you can overcome.

Success isn't about giving what you've got; it's about giving *everything it takes*. When you commit fully, the Universe conspires to help you. Even when it seems like everything is falling apart, unseen forces are coming together to support you. When you pour your heart into your efforts, the Universe matches your commitment.

Here is a beautiful story that illustrates this principle. It's adapted from a fable by Swami Paramahansa Yogananda, and it's called

Two Frogs in Trouble

One sunny day, Big Frog and Little Frog were hopping along when they accidentally tumbled into a bucket of fresh milk. Panic set in as they realized the sides were too slippery to climb. They began paddling frantically, trying to stay afloat.

Their fellow frogs gathered around the bucket, watching the spectacle. Instead of offering encouragement, they shouted discouraging words: "It's hopeless! Why bother? Just give up!"

As time passed, Big Frog grew tired. The constant paddling and the negative comments wore him down. "What's the point?" he sighed, giving in to despair. He stopped paddling and sank to the bottom.

But Little Frog wasn't ready to quit. Ignoring the taunts, he focused on survival. He kept paddling, determined to overcome this challenge.

As the hours ticked by, the milk began to thicken, making it harder to swim. Little Frog's legs were almost paralyzed with exhaustion. It seemed like he couldn't last much longer. But a thought kept him going: "Giving up is like being dead. I'll keep swimming as long as I can. While there's life, there's hope."

With renewed determination, Little Frog churned the milk into waves. Just when he thought all hope was lost, he felt something solid beneath his feet. To his amazement, his constant paddling had churned the milk into butter! He leaped onto this self-made platform and out of the bucket to freedom.

Now, you might think the difference between Little Frog and Big Frog was simply that Little Frog had more heart and more determination. And you'd be partly right. But there was another crucial difference – Little Frog was deaf. He couldn't hear the discouraging words from the other frogs. In fact, he thought they were cheering him on: "Keep going, Little Frog! You can do it!"

This story teaches us a powerful lesson: persistence is the key to success. But it also shows us the importance of our mindset. Even when faced with negativity, focusing on encouragement – whether it's real or something we create in our minds – can fuel our perseverance and lead us to success.

Etch this profound truth in your memory: The Universe only fully releases her rewards *after* you refuse to quit! Rest assured that the Universe will test your resolve. She'll push you, maybe even break you a little, just to see if you'll weather the storm.

As you work toward your goals, you'll encounter people who try to bring you down. Some may do it intentionally, others unintentionally. But here's where your true strength comes into play: you don't have to listen to them. Tune them out like static on a broken radio. Instead, listen to the voice within that says, "Keep pushing. This is your path. You've got what it takes." And, when times get tough, let this poem inspire you:

Don't Quit

When things go wrong as they sometimes will;
When the road you're trudging seems all uphill;
When the funds are low, and the debts are high
And you want to smile, but have to sigh;

When care is pressing you down a bit
Rest if you must, but do not quit.

Success is failure turned inside out;
The silver tint of the clouds of doubt;
And you can never tell how close you are
It may be near when it seems so far.
So stick to the fight when you're hardest hit
It's when things go wrong that you must not quit!

Staying determined and resilient is essential as you pursue your dreams. Focus on your goals, as this will keep you motivated even when challenges arise. It will give you a sense of direction and purpose, helping you push through tough times.

Sometimes, when things seem at their worst, the best thing you can do is hang in there and wait for your opportunity. Like a ship in a storm, keep heading toward your goal. The storm will pass, and soon, you'll find yourself at your destination, filled with a sense of accomplishment that only those who persist can feel.

Life is full of surprises, and circumstances can change, requiring flexibility in your approach. Being flexible doesn't mean giving up on your dreams; it means finding new ways to achieve them. Sometimes, you may need to adjust your sails to keep moving forward.

The only way to fail is to quit. Failure isn't final; it's an opportunity to learn. When you fail, take a moment to understand what went wrong. Every successful person has experienced failure, but the key is to learn from it and keep going.

As Elbert Hubbard wisely said, *"There is no failure except in no longer trying."* Persistence is its own reward. Many people don't realize how close they were to success when they gave up. So never give in, and never, ever give up!

If you ever feel like quitting, think of diamonds. Here's a beautiful poem to remind you of the power of persistence:

Stick to Your Job

Diamonds are only chunks of coal
That stuck to their jobs, you see;
If they'd petered out, as most of us do,
Where would the diamonds be?

It isn't the fact of making a start,
It's the sticking that counts, I'll say;
It's the fellow that knows not the meaning of fail,
But hammers and hammers away.

Whenever you think that you've come to the end,
And you're beaten as bad as can be,
Remember that diamonds are chunks of coal
That stuck to their jobs, you see.

~ Minnie Richard Smith (1922)

Failure comes from taking the path of least persistence. Stay committed to your cause and be optimistic. See every challenge as an opportunity because hidden in adversity are the most important lessons.

Emmet Fox shared a powerful insight:

Any difficulties that come to you, no matter what they are, must be exactly what you need at that moment to enable you to take the next step forward by overcoming them. The only real misfortune is suffering without learning the lesson.

Know that you are a winner. You've already faced and overcome some of life's greatest challenges – learning to walk, talk, read, and write. Each of these skills took thousands of attempts to master.

Do you know what it takes to learn to walk, let alone to learn to talk, read, or write in a particular language? Scientists tell us that learning to walk is quite a feat. It requires thousands of attempts at integrating multiple skills into a coherent whole. Coordinating the dozens of muscles needed to balance ourselves upright and then propel ourselves forward using our legs alternately is an extraordinarily complicated process. Yet, we did it. It took time and practice, but we mastered the skill and surpassed it by learning to run, skip, jump, dance, and more.

Ponder it for a moment. You learned to crawl and then to stand on those two wobbly feet after falling on your bottom countless times. Then you took those few tentative steps and stumbled and fell again, countless times. If you had a time-lapse video of every time you fell and got up again while learning to walk, you'd never be discouraged by the pitifully small obstacles you've got in front of you at the moment.

And you even got hurt in the process! You cried sometimes, but you never gave up. Regardless of the ongoing failures, you never faltered in your determination to walk. You never judged yourself for your failures. Instead, you kept trying. You faced the risks and mastered the skill. Congratulations!

Think about that determination. *You've proven many times that you have what it takes to succeed.* So don't stop now. Pursue your dream relentlessly, and never give up! Success comes to those who stay with their dreams long enough to reach them.

Let these powerful words from Theodore Roosevelt's "Citizenship in a Republic" speech inspire you:

The Man in the Arena

"It is not the critic who counts; not the man who points out how the strong man stumbles, or where the doer of deeds could have done them better. The credit belongs to the man who is actually in the arena, whose face is marred by dust and sweat and blood; who strives valiantly; who errs, who comes short again and again, because there is no effort without error and shortcoming; but who does actually strive to do the deeds; who knows great enthusiasms, the great devotions; who spends himself in a worthy cause; who at the best knows in the end the triumph of high achievement, and who at the worst, if he fails, at least fails while daring greatly, so that his place shall never be with those cold and timid souls who neither know victory nor defeat."

~ Theodore Roosevelt, "Citizenship In A Republic," 1910

Your journey to success is one-of-a-kind, brimming with challenges that will shape you. Every step forward brings you closer to your dreams. The Universe helps those who relentlessly pursue their goals. So, move forward with courage, determination, and belief in yourself.

You possess the incredible power to overcome any obstacle, learn any skill, and achieve any goal. Your success story is waiting to be written; only you can write it. So, take that first step, keep moving forward, and never, never, never give up. Your future self will thank you for the persistence and dedication you show today.

Hidden truths:

1. Successful people use leverage extensively.
2. Negative self-talk sabotages the very success that you seek.
3. Being focused is to be single-minded in the pursuit of your outcomes.

4. Most people would prefer to see you fail rather than succeed.
5. Success likes speed – the strategy should be: 'Ready, Fire, Aim'.
6. You must be willing to pay an opportunity cost – give up a portion of those things that you want most, such as time or money.
7. If you want to be in the top 1% in your field, you must do what the other 99% are not doing.
8. Life is a succession of events. What matters is how we deal with events.
9. Success comes at a price – you must be willing to do everything necessary to achieve your outcome.
10. The Universe only fully releases her rewards *after* you refuse to quit!

PART 4

The Law of Receiving

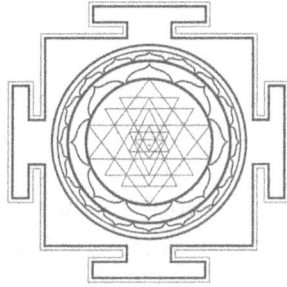

Chapter 11

Having What You Want

Turning your wildest dreams into reality – that's the essence of manifestation, and it's not as far-fetched as it might sound. The secret lies in understanding the powerful interplay between *"being"* and *"doing."* Consider them a power duo, working together for your highest good. What you embody (your being) sets the tone, while your actions (the doing) give it form. Together, they shape your reality and determine what you can *have* in life.

Recall this profound truth: you don't just attract what you want; you attract what you *are*. You are a living, breathing energy field. This energy acts like a magnet, drawing experiences and results into your life. Want to attract something amazing? You've got to match its energy – vibrate on its wavelength. It's similar to tuning a radio – when you're on the right frequency, the music comes through loud and clear.

Changing your inner world is the key to changing your outer reality. It's about becoming the person who already has what you desire and taking consistent actions that reflect this new identity. By focusing on *being* and *doing*, you raise your level of consciousness and become a living embodiment of your aspirations. This is the golden ticket to *having* what you want.

11.1 The 'Threshold Factor' of Success

Picture success as a boiling pot of water. Just as water needs to reach 100°C (212°F) to boil, your consciousness must reach a specific threshold to manifest your desires. We call this the 'Threshold Factor' of success.

This Threshold Factor is the tipping point where your efforts culminate in tangible results. It's when your consciousness, thoughts, feelings, and actions align with your desires, allowing the Universe to bring them to fruition. Think of it as a cosmic scoreboard, where you must earn a certain number of points before the Universe awards your prize. It's similar to collecting points in a rewards program, where you can trade them for cool stuff like cash, discounts, coupons, and other free items.

The Success Continuum and Goodwill Points

Success Continuum ®

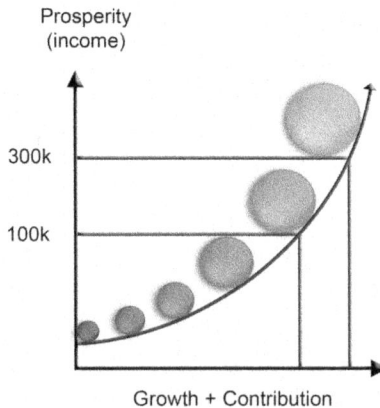

Your journey along the Success Continuum® depends on two crucial factors: growth and contribution. Growth and contribution represent your input (*being* and *doing*), while prosperity is your output (*having*). The more you put in, the more you get out – it's that simple.

Let's consider your journey toward success using the metaphor of a Universal Goodwill Account. As you grow and contribute, you're essentially depositing "Goodwill Points" into this cosmic bank account. Positive thoughts, feelings, and actions boost your balance, propelling you forward on the Success Continuum®. Conversely, negative behaviors – like selfishness, worry, or resentment – act like withdrawals, causing you to slide backward.

Your position on this continuum reflects your current level of consciousness and, by extension, your measure of prosperity. If you haven't yet manifested your desire, it simply means you haven't reached the required threshold of Goodwill Points.

Keep in mind, only the Universe (or God, if you prefer) decides when you've accumulated enough Goodwill Points to vibrationally align with and attract your desired outcome. Your job is to keep adding to your account through positive thoughts and actions.

The Power of Universal Laws

Now, here's where it gets really exciting. The speed at which you accumulate Goodwill Points depends on how well you apply the Laws of the Universe. Just as money serves as the currency of exchange in our material world, energy is the currency of exchange in the Universe. Money is spent to acquire material goods or services; energy is "spent" on thoughts, actions, and feelings that can attract or create desired outcomes. Just as money comes in different denominations, Goodwill Points (which are earned through the expenditure of energy) can be accumulated in varying quantities – small or large, slowly over time, or in rapid bursts. The key to fast-tracking your manifestations is to accumulate large quantities of Goodwill Points as quickly as possible.

Let's break this down with some examples:

1. The Law of Giving: This law suggests that you earn extra points when you give more, especially when you give selflessly. Envision it as a cosmic bonus system – the more you give, the more you receive. You might even earn additional points when you give what

The Inexplicable Laws of Success

you need most. Remember John Harricharan's story about "The Power of Giving" from chapter 9.6? That's a perfect illustration of this principle in action.

2. The Law of Risk: This law implies that those taking calculated risks often enjoy higher rewards. Think of successful investors who might make losses on several investments before striking gold, or oil companies that drill multiple dry wells before finding a 'gusher.' The key here is that the eventual gains tend to far outweigh the losses. It's comparable to playing a high-stakes game where the jackpot is exponentially larger than your initial investment.

3. The Law of Faith: This law acts as a multiplier for your Goodwill Points. When you have unflinching faith in your desired outcome, it's akin to applying a power boost to your efforts. It amplifies the value of every action you take.

4. The Law of Gratitude: Expressing gratitude in advance for your desired outcome is like adding a turbo-charger to your manifestation engine. It multiplies your Goodwill Points, accelerating your progress toward your tipping point.

5. The Law of Emotion: Adding intense emotion to your desires and actions is like pouring rocket fuel into your manifestation vehicle. It supercharges your Goodwill Points, dramatically shortening the distance between you and your goals.

Now, imagine combining these laws. Let's say you take a significant risk (Law of Risk), approach it with unshakable faith (Law of Faith), express gratitude for the outcome before it happens (Law of Gratitude), and infuse the whole process with intense positive emotion (Law of Emotion). You've just created a perfect storm of manifestation, multiplying your Goodwill Points exponentially and rocketing towards your tipping point!

The laws of the universe are complex and interconnected. While we may not always understand the full value of our actions or how exactly these laws interplay, one thing is crystal clear: *everything counts*. Each thought, word, and deed is either a deposit or withdrawal in your Universal Goodwill Account.

The Balloon Analogy

To better understand the process of reaching your Threshold Factor, imagine your goal as a balloon that needs to be inflated until it bursts – that's your threshold point. Every positive action you take, every universal law you apply successfully, is like a breath of air inflating this balloon.

But, here's the catch: life's challenges and negative experiences create tiny pinholes in your balloon. These allow air (energy) to escape, slowly decreasing the balance in your Goodwill Account. It's like trying to fill a leaky bucket – you need to pour in water faster than it's leaking out.

To reach your goal, you must maintain momentum and keep inflating the balloon faster than it can deflate. This requires consistent effort, positive energy, and a deep understanding of the universal laws that govern manifestation. If you stop or slow down, the balloon will deflate, and you'll never reach the bursting point – your desired outcome.

See it as a cosmic tug-of-war between you and the Universe. The Universe is constantly pulling on the balloon, trying to deflate it through life's challenges and obstacles – recall the story of Soichiro Honda from chapter 10.8. But you can counteract this by putting in more energy and effort than the Universe is dissipating. By doing so, you'll eventually reach your threshold of success and manifest your desires.

This analogy underscores the importance of consistency and persistence in your journey along the Success Continuum. It's not enough to make sporadic deposits into your Goodwill Account; you need to maintain a steady flow of positive energy to overcome the natural tendency (in life) for things to slow down or fall apart.

The key is to maintain momentum and keep inflating your balloon of success. With every positive action and effective application of the universal laws, you're inching closer to your goal. Even when faced with setbacks or challenges, keep pushing forward. The air may leak out slowly, but your consistent efforts will ensure you always gain ground.

So, keep playing this cosmic game with enthusiasm, faith, and relentless determination. The Universe is keeping score, and with every deposit into your Goodwill Account, you're one step closer to bursting that balloon and achieving your wildest dreams. Your success is not just possible – it's inevitable, as long as you keep inflating that balloon with willful persistence and positive energy.

11.2   The Ultimate Success Formula®

What is the formula for success? While many paths lead to success, there's no one-size-fits-all approach to success. Nevertheless, certain key factors are common across all achievements. Our Ultimate Success Formula® incorporates these essential components: Image, Energy, Emotion, and Teamwork. Let's break it down:

Image (I)

Success begins in the mind. You must first envision your desired outcome in vivid detail before it can manifest in reality. This mental image acts as a blueprint that the Universe uses to attract the necessary resources and opportunities.

Visualization isn't just a feel-good exercise – when you consistently hold an image in your mind, it always seeks expression in the physical world.

Energy (E)

Everything in the universe is energy, including your thoughts, feelings, and actions. The energy you expend in pursuit of your goals is the raw material of manifestation. Generally, the more positive energy you invest, the sooner you'll see results.

Remember, your energy output directly influences your position on the Success Continuum®. Consistently putting out positive energy aligns your subconscious mind with your conscious desires, accelerating your progress toward your goals.

Team (T)

No one achieves greatness alone. Your team represents the power of collaboration – the individuals who support and assist you in realizing your vision. A strong team provides diverse skills, perspectives, and resources that amplify your efforts.

As the saying goes, "None of us is as smart as all of us." Therefore, make the most of the power of teamwork to accelerate your progress.

Emotion (e)

Emotion is the fuel that powers your journey to success. It acts as a multiplier, determining the intensity and effectiveness of your efforts. The more emotionally invested you are in your goal, the higher your vibrational frequency, and the more rapidly you'll attract the necessary elements for success.

Passion and emotional commitment are what keep you going when obstacles arise. They provide the resilience needed to persist until you succeed.

The Formula in Action

Putting it all together, our Ultimate Success Formula® can be expressed as:

$$I^e + E^e + T = S$$

In other words, Success (S) is the result of a clear Image (I) of your desired outcome powered by intense Emotion (e), combined with the necessary Energy (E) to achieve it, also powered by intense Emotion (e), plus the support of your Team (T).

The story of Sir Edmund Hillary perfectly illustrates the Ultimate Success Formula® in action.

Edmund Hillary's Everest Triumph

On May 29, 1953, New Zealand's Edmund Hillary and Nepalese Sherpa Tenzing Norgay became legends as the first climbers to summit Mount Everest, the Earth's highest peak at an astounding 8,848 meters (29,032 feet). This monumental achievement thrust Hillary into international fame and earned him a knighthood – he became Sir Edmund Hillary practically overnight. Yet, his ascent mirrored a profound personal journey that demanded resilience and unshakable determination.

The summit of Everest had claimed numerous expeditions since 1922, and failure was a familiar tale before Hillary's triumphant ascent in 1953. He himself had faced setbacks in two previous attempts. In 1951, a British reconnaissance expedition to Everest fell short of its goal. The following year, Hillary joined another expedition targeting Cho Oyu, a Himalayan peak west of Everest, but that attempt was also thwarted due to a lack of a viable route on the Nepalese side.

Despite these setbacks, Hillary was invited to speak in England. As he stepped onto the stage to thunderous applause, a strange dissonance filled him. The audience celebrated his attempts at greatness, yet Hillary felt undeserving; he had not yet conquered Everest.

In a pivotal moment during his speech, Hillary stepped away from the microphone, his gaze fixed on a picture of Everest adorning the wall. With a defiant gesture, he pointed his clenched fist at the image and declared, "Mount Everest, you beat me the first time, but I'll beat you the next time because you've grown all you are ever going to grow, and I'm still growing."

This powerful declaration embodied Hillary's tenacious spirit and set the stage for his eventual triumph. A year later, he became the first person to conquer Mount Everest, the tallest mountain in the world!

Let's break down how Hillary applied the Ultimate Success Formula®:

1. **Image (I)**: Hillary had a clear *image* of himself standing atop Everest long before it finally manifested.
2. **Energy (E)**: Despite years of seemingly insurmountable challenges, he invested significant *energy* into his relentless pursuit of the summit.
3. **Team (T)**: His expedition involved over 400 individuals, including 362 porters and 20 local guides – a true *team* effort.
4. **Emotion (e)**: Hillary possessed a burning desire – an intense *emotion* driving him forward. This emotion amplified his vision (I^e) and the energy (E^e) he invested in pursuing his goal.
5. **Success (S)**: Given Hillary's effective application of the formula, his Success (S) was inevitable. He was the first to conquer the 'Mighty Everest.'

Your Journey to Success

The *Ultimate Success Formula®* isn't just some abstract idea – it's a hands-on blueprint to reshape how you approach achievement. When you apply it consistently, something incredible happens: your thoughts, emotions, and actions synchronize with your goals. This alignment becomes a kind of magnetic energy, pulling you closer to what you desire.

But here's the twist: while your effort is indispensable, the timing isn't entirely in your hands. The greater force – Universal Consciousness – decides when you've truly hit the sweet spot. Your role? Show up relentlessly, give it your all – 'do whatever it takes' – and trust the process.

So, moving forward, make the *Ultimate Success Formula*® your mantra. Live in tune with universal laws, stay patient yet persistent, and watch how the doors to your deepest dreams swing open – often in ways you didn't expect.

Hidden Truths:

1. Having is the consequence of being and doing.
2. Everything counts. Every thought, word, or deed either helps you or hinders you.
3. To realize a desired outcome, you need to reach a specific threshold or 'tipping point' in terms of your level of consciousness.
4. If you go too slow or stop working towards your goal, you will retrogress to the starting point.
5. To attain your goal you must constantly be putting in more energy than the Universe is dissipating.
6. You must see your goal completed in all its glory in your mind before you will experience it in your outer world.

Chapter 12

Your Moment of Truth – Embracing Transformation

As you reach the final pages of this book, you're standing at a crossroads – a *turning point* that demands more of you than passive reflection. The insights you've gathered here aren't just ideas; they're the keys to releasing your limitless potential. This is your *moment of truth*. Will you continue on autopilot, sticking to the familiar, or will you seize this moment to embrace the transformative power within you?

But let's be clear – transformation isn't just another word for change. It's deeper and more demanding. It's about *growth* that stretches your limits, raises your level of consciousness, and brings your beliefs and actions into harmony with the natural laws of the Universe. As you internalize these principles, they'll rewire the way you see the world, shaping you into a more *valuable* and *fulfilled* version of yourself.

And yes, growth isn't cozy – it can be downright uncomfortable. But here's the truth: you can't rise to new levels by simply absorbing knowledge. Real progress demands action, a willingness to push past your comfort zone, and the courage to face challenges head-on. This is how you activate the Law of Receiving, shifting your energy and attracting the outcomes you have positioned yourself to receive.

Life presents many turning points. At each of these moments, we face a decision. A wise Turkish proverb reminds us: *"No matter how far you have gone on the wrong road, turn back."* It's never too late to start again, no matter how difficult it seems. The following Sufi tale beautifully illustrates this:

The Stream of Life

A stream, born in distant mountains, traveled across varied landscapes until it reached the sands of the desert. It had overcome every obstacle thus far, so it believed it could conquer this one, too. Yet, as the stream poured into the desert, its waters vanished into the sands. The stream felt certain its destiny was to cross the desert and reach the sea, but no matter what it tried, it seemed there was no way forward.

Before long, the stream heard a voice whispering from the desert itself, "The wind crosses the desert, so can you."

"Yes, but the wind can fly!" the stream cried, still throwing itself into the sands.

"You'll never get across that way," the desert whispered once again. "You'll have to let the wind carry you."

"But how?" cried out the stream.

"You have to let the wind absorb you."

The stream balked at the idea. It had never been absorbed before; it didn't want to lose its identity. "If I give myself to the wind, how can I know I will ever be a stream again?"

"The wind," replied the desert, "carries water over the desert and then releases it as rain. Falling again, the water becomes a river once more."

The desert warned that the stream could choose to continue flowing into the sands, but that would eventually lead to it becoming a swamp or a stagnant puddle. It could never cross the desert by remaining as it was.

The stream protested: "Why can't I remain as I am?"

"You cannot stay the same," replied the desert. "Either you give yourself to the wind or become a swamp. By surrendering to the wind, your essential part will be carried away and reborn as a stream on the other side."

The stream could not believe it but realized that the best that could be attained without attempting the suggestion would be to become a swamp. Either way, the stream could not stay as it was.

The stream hesitated. Silently, it listened to its inner voice, remembering ancient memories of once being held by the wind. Finally, the stream surrendered to the sun's heat, allowing its vapors to rise into the welcoming embrace of the wind. It was carried in great white clouds over the desert. The water returned as gentle rain on the far side, trickling down rocky slopes. Gradually, it gained strength, flowing as a swift stream toward the sea.

~ Adapted from *Tales of the Dervishes* (Idries Shah)

Like the stream finding its way through the vast, unyielding desert, you are a fluid current of consciousness, constantly shifting, always evolving. Life doesn't wait or remain static; it calls on you to adapt, to shape yourself in response to every twist, turn, and challenge that arises. The beauty of this lies in your ability to transform.

Just as the stream had to completely reinvent itself – changing from liquid to vapor and back again – your journey of growth often requires reinventing yourself, seeing your challenges and opportunities through new eyes. This willingness to reinvent yourself, to let go of old patterns, and to embrace new ways of being is the true key to unlocking your potential for growth.

Real transformation isn't just about persistence – it's about surrendering to evolution, embracing the unknown, and trusting that every shift brings you closer to the person you're meant to become.

Be the Change

As Mahatma Gandhi wisely said,

Be the change you want to see in life.

This is it – your defining moment. Will you choose to transform yourself and, through that shift, the world around you? It's a powerful decision, one that ripples far beyond what you can see. Every action you take, every thought you conceive, and every word you release into the world creates energy waves, touching places you may never even know exist.

When you strive for greatness, living deliberately and with purpose, you're doing more than shaping your personal story. You're becoming a catalyst for something far more significant, a force that contributes to the collective advancement of humanity. Your transformation isn't just yours; it's a spark that lights countless others.

Everything in nature grows and evolves. A seed becomes a tree, creating more seeds and continuing the cycle of life indefinitely. You are an integral part of the universal cycle of growth and expansion. Your purpose is twofold:

1. Become all that you can be (grow)
2. Use your unique talents to make this world better (contribute)

As Woodrow Wilson eloquently put it:

> *You are not here merely to make a living. You are here in order to enable the world to live more amply, with greater vision, with a finer spirit of hope and achievement. You are here to enrich the world, and you impoverish yourself if you forget the errand.*

Dare To Succeed

You now realize that you're not just a spectator in this world – you're an active co-creator, molding reality with every thought, every action, and every choice you make. Where once you saw limitations, you now see opportunities. Where once you felt fear, you now feel enthusiasm. The world hasn't changed, but your perspective has, revealing infinite possibilities for expressing yourself.

So, make your life matter. Find something meaningful to strive for – something bigger than yourself. Don't let another moment slip away. Don't settle for less than you're capable of achieving.

As you close this book, carry with you these essential truths:

1. You are capable of constant growth and change.
2. You cannot attract a different outcome with the same energy that created your present circumstance.
3. There is no limit to how much you can be, do, and have. The only requirement is that you engage life with passion and express yourself at a higher level of consciousness.

Throughout this book, we've explored the inexplicable laws that govern success and fulfillment. As we conclude our journey together, I'd like to share a poem that distills these essential truths into a simple yet powerful reminder of how the game of life is meant to be played:

The Rules of the Game

Life is a game, a journey we're born to play,
With rules that govern every step of the way.
You can choose to win or lose, it's up to you,
Your unique approach is how you break through.

The rules are shrouded in mystery, sometimes unclear,
But one thing's certain: your actions will bring you near
To victory or defeat. The choice is always yours,
But be warned, you cannot defy Universal laws.

Often you may declare you're doing all you can do,
But your results will reveal, that's not entirely true.
For every breach of the rules, you'll pay the price,
And repeat the hard lesson, till you learn it twice.

But don't be discouraged, for every setback's a test,
A chance to learn, to grow, and to do your best.
For only when you've mastered the rules of the game,
Will you emerge victorious, with a life truly yours to claim.

So, play the game of life with intention and might,
Apply the rules with wisdom, and shine with all your light.
For in the end, it's not just about winning or losing the fight,
But about living a life that's authentic, meaningful, and bright.

~ Verusha Robbins

Life is in session *now*. It's time to shine, make your mark, and turn your dreams into reality. Let today be the turning point in your life when transformation occurs within you, and you're never the same again. Embrace the changes that are on the horizon, and let your life become living proof of the power of growth and the infinite possibilities that arise when you dare to dream.

Your future is in your hands. Go forward with courage, determination, and a deep belief in your potential. The world is eager to witness the unique contribution that only you can make. It's time to let your light illuminate the way for others.

The first step? It's small yet momentous. Take it today. As you do, watch the Universe fall into rhythm with your efforts, guiding you closer to your aspirations.

The Universe is whispering, *"Welcome home."* Your transformation begins now, leading to a new you – one that is more aligned, more aware, and more capable than ever before. *This is your new consciousness!*

A BIG Favor, please!

Dear Reader,

It's great to see you finish *The Inexplicable Laws of Success*. In a world that often rushes past life's deeper truths, we're thrilled to offer insights that help people pause, reflect, and thrive. Hopefully, this book has added some wisdom to enrich your journey through life.

Your thoughts on the book would be greatly appreciated. They are not just feedback – they're a guiding light for others finding their own paths toward growth. A single review might seem like a drop in the ocean, but it carries immense weight. In today's busy world, reviews often get overlooked. It's easy to think someone else will do it, or that your voice doesn't matter. But the truth is, *your voice has immense power.*

Imagine if you inspired someone else's transformation through your words. That simple action could stretch farther than you'd ever guess, influencing lives you'll never even meet!

Better still… what if you gifted the **free** version of this book to someone you care about? Think of it as planting a seed in their life. These principles could be the exact reminder they need to rediscover their strength and their *why*. It's like handing someone a flashlight for the moments when life feels a little dark. That one gift could inspire changes in them – and by extension, in everyone they touch. Maybe even you, in ways you wouldn't expect.

Want to help others? It's simple:

1. Visit Amazon or Chosen4u.com/TilosEpub/.
2. Search for *The Inexplicable Laws of Success*.
3. Scroll down to "Customer reviews," click "Write a customer review," and share your honest thoughts.

4.   Share the **free** e-book/e-pub link with your circle – they might be waiting for just this kind of nudge and would appreciate your kind gesture.

Every step you take in sharing this message multiplies positive change, inspiring countless others. We're deeply grateful for your support and for joining us in this mission to create a brighter, more empowered world.

With heartfelt appreciation,
Verusha & Virend

P.S. If this book has sparked your curiosity for more of life's invaluable lessons, you'll love *"100+ Inspirational Short Stories about Success and Happiness"* and *"100+ Inspirational Poems and Prose about Life and Success."* They offer even more wisdom and inspiration to uplift and empower you.

Other resources by Verusha & Virend

100+ Inspirational Short Stories about Success and Happiness: Insightful Words of Wisdom to Motivate, Educate and Create a More Empowered You. Everyone, at some point in their lives, feels overwhelmed by the challenges and obstacles they have to face. In times of difficulty, we often look around to find a source of inspiration and hope. Sometimes, the easiest and most powerful way to get a message across is through a story. Stories hold our attention and stay with us long after we have heard them. 100+ Inspirational Short Stories about Success and Happiness will inspire and uplift readers with its stories of optimism, faith, and strength.

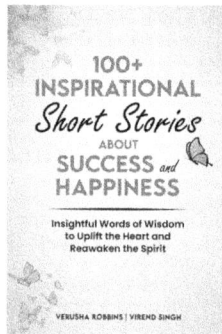

100+
INSPIRATIONAL
Short Stories
ABOUT
SUCCESS *and*
HAPPINESS

Insightful Words of Wisdom
to Uplift the Heart and
Reawaken the Spirit

VERUSHA ROBBINS | VIREND SINGH

100+ Inspirational Poems and Prose about Life and Success: Thought-provoking and Empowering Words to Uplift and Inspire You contains an impressive collection of insightful poetry that will touch your heart, give you hope, and motivate you to be your best. The poems provide a powerful source of wisdom and inspiration and will make a great addition to any self-improvement or motivational book collection. It is a great resource for speakers, coaches, teachers, leaders, and parents.

100+
INSPIRATIONAL
Poems and Prose
ABOUT
LIFE *and* SUCCESS

Thought-provoking and Empowering
Words to Uplift and Inspire You

VERUSHA ROBBINS | VIREND SINGH

Inspirational Words and Positive Quotes to Live By: An Insightful Collection of Motivational Quotes is packed with wisdom and serves to remind you that life can be good, no matter what challenges you may be facing. These quotes will empower and encourage you to live your life to the fullest. They come from accomplished people, sages, philosophers, and thinkers, all of whom started out as ordinary citizens and have achieved greatness.

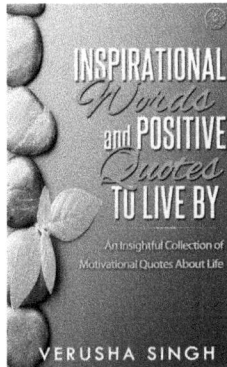

For other resources by Verusha and Virend go to
www.inkNivory.com/resources/
www.CoolSelfHelpTips.com

Our Gifts to You

If you enjoyed this book, then you will find the following FREE publications just as enjoyable:

- The 12 Best Inspirational Poems about Life and Success
- The 10 Best Motivational Stories to Uplift and Inspire
- Rise and Shine: My Journey to a Better Me – a short 12-module online course comprising a guide, printable journal, and monthly planner for each module

Go to www.Chosen4U.com/GiftsSS/ to get free access now.

About The Authors

This book is the collaborative effort of Virend and Verusha, a father and daughter team.

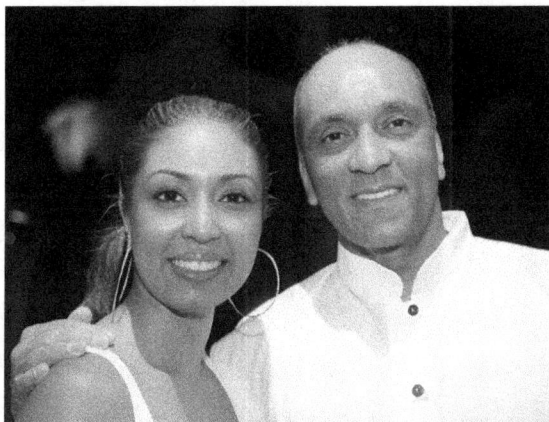

Verusha Robbins is an accomplished writer and entrepreneur who thrives at both, captivating audiences with fictional narratives that entertain, as well as empowering others through personal transformation. Her expertise in Media & Writing, and Editing & Publishing fuels her success in both realms. Her professional journey includes pivotal roles at esteemed publishing companies like Hay House (Australia). Looking ahead, Verusha remains committed to weaving captivating worlds through fiction while equipping readers with the knowledge they need to flourish in all aspects of life.

Virend Singh, a seasoned entrepreneur with an MBA, leverages his years of experience to empower others. His journey, marked by both triumphs and challenges, has instilled in him a deep understanding of the mindset and behaviors that drive high achievers. Drawing on these firsthand insights, Virend collaborates with his daughter, Verusha, in a unique father-daughter team. Together, they empower individuals to unlock their full potential, achieving success in both personal and professional spheres.

For fans of fantasy...

If you are drawn to fantasy, in particular dark romance fantasy, then you will truly enjoy Verusha's latest novels:

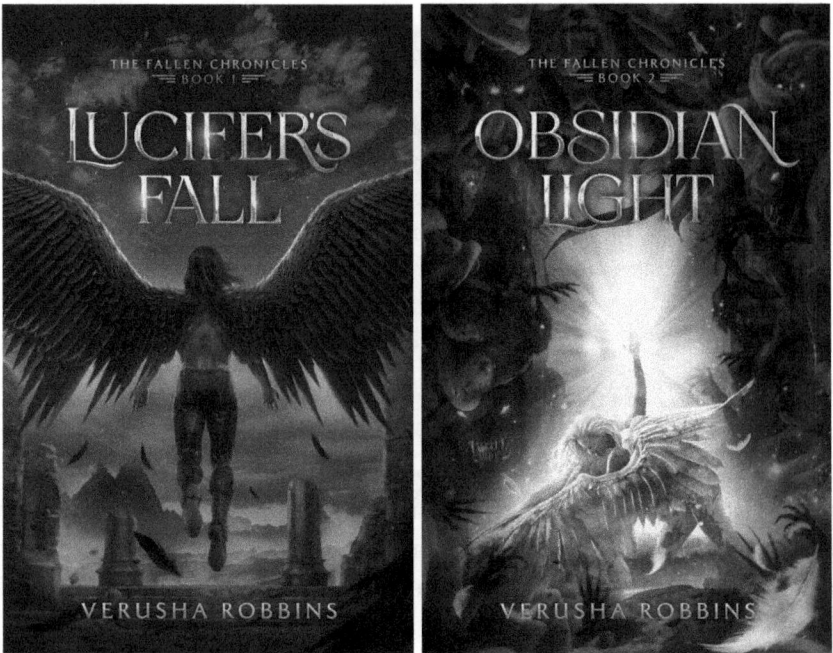

If you love the intricate world-building in Sarah J. Maas, Carissa Broadbent, and Anne Bishop's works, prepare to be mesmerized by these books.

Step into a spellbinding realm where angels and demons clash in an epic saga. Sandriel, a fallen angel with a mysterious past, is ensnared in a perilous dance with Lucifer, the most mesmerizing fallen angel of all. Her mission is clear: rescue the captive warrior angels in Hell and combat the Fallen, all while resisting the overwhelming allure of the Devil himself.

Themes to Captivate You:

- Enemies to Lovers
- Hell and Angels
- Captivity and Liberation
- Greek Mythology
- Emotional Healing and Scars
- Revenge and Redemption

Prepare for an exhilarating journey brimming with multifaceted characters, forbidden love, and jaw-dropping twists that will keep you reading late into the night.

Readers are enthralled by "Lucifer's Fall" and "Obsidian Light":

- "A masterpiece of storytelling. I couldn't put it down!"
- "The twists and turns are mind-blowing!"
- "I haven't been this captivated by a book in years!"
- "This book is 'unputdownable,' unique, and mysteriously beautiful."

Free Sample Available!

Download the first six chapters of "Lucifer's Fall" for free and discover why readers can't get enough. Visit www.chosen4u.com/LF6

Available now on all major platforms.

The following are registered trademarks of Virend Singh and Verusha Robbins.

Success Continuum ®

Prosperity
(income)

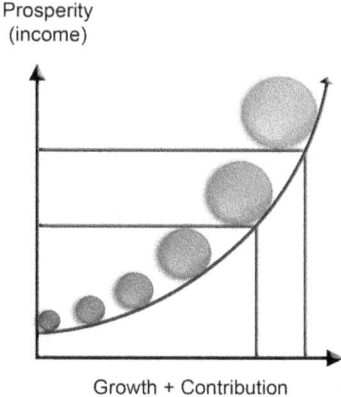

Growth + Contribution

Ultimate Success Formula ®

$$I^e + E^e + T = S$$

References

Books:

Allen, J (1948). *As a Man Thinketh*. DeVorss & Company.

Braden, G (2006). *Secrets of the Lost Mode of Prayer: The Hidden Power of Beauty, Blessings, Wisdom, and Hurt*. San Diego: Hay House.

Chopra, D (1993). *Creating Affluence: Wealth Consciousness in the Field of All Possibilities*. New World Library Walk Your Talk With Praxis / Amber-Allen Publishing.

Chopra, D (1994). *The Seven Spiritual Laws of Success: A Practical Guide to the Fulfillment of Your Dreams*. New World Library / Amber-Allen Publishing.

Coelho, P (1995). *The Alchemist: A Fable About Following Your Dream*. 16th ed. Harper SanFrancisco.

Covey, Stephen R. (1990). *The 7 Habits of Highly Effective People*. Free Press.

Dyer, W (2004). *The Power of Intention*.: Hay House.

Gibson, R (1998). *Rethinking the Future: Rethinking Business, Principles, Competition, Control & Complexity, Leadership, Market, and the World*. Nicholas Brealey Publishing.

Halberstam, Y and Leventhal, J (1997). *Small Miracles: Extraordinary Coincidences from Everyday Life*. Adams Media Corporation. p18-19.

Harvey, E and Ventura, S (1996). *Walk Awhile In My Shoes: Gut Level, Real-World Messages Between Managers and Employees* . Walk the Talk.

Hawkins, David R (2001). *The Eye of the I: From Which Nothing Is Hidden*. 2nd ed. Veritas Publishing

Hill, N (1986). *Think and Grow Rich*. Ballantine Books.

Kersey, C (1998). *Unstoppable: 45 Powerful Stories of Perseverance and Triumph from People Just Like You*. Sourcebooks, Inc.

Maltz, M (1989). *Psycho-Cybernetics, A New Way to Get More Living Out of Life*. London: Pocket Books. p12-13.

Murphy, J (2001). *The Power of Your Subconscious Mind*. Bantam.

Peale, N V (1996). *The Power of Positive Thinking*. Ballantine Books.

Pearsall, P (1999). *The Heart's Code: Tapping the Wisdom and Power of Our Heart Energy*. Broadway Books.

Ramsey, Dave (2003). *The Total Money Makeover: A Proven Plan for Financial Fitness*. Thomas Nelson.

Scovel-Shinn, F (2004). *The Game of Life and How to Play It*. London: Random House UK.

Tracy, B (2009). *Reinvention: How to Make the Rest of Your Life the Best of Your Life*. AMACOM.

Tracy, B (2008). *Flight Plan: The Real Secret of Success*. Berrett-Koehler Publishers.

Tracy, B (2001). *The 21 Success Secrets of Self-Made Millionaires*. Berrett-Koehler Publishers.

Wattles D, W (2002). *The Science of Getting Rich or Financial Success Through Creative Thought*. 4th ed. Iceni Books.

Yogananda, P (1946). *Autobiography of a Yogi*. Self-Realization Fellowship.

Internet References:

Baba, Sai. (2005). *Suitable Hiding Place.* Available: http://groups.yahoo.com/group/saibabanews/message/7356. Last accessed 3rd November 2011.

Batterson, M. (2005). *The Positive Paradigm.* Available: http://www.markbatterson.com/uncategorized/the-positive-paradigm/. Last accessed 14 April 2011.

Dyer, W. (2011). *Your Impact On The Consciousness Of Humanity.* Available: http://www.ownyourreality.com/mind-power-articles/your_impact_on_the_consciousness_of_humanity.html. Last accessed 8th Jan 2012.

Harricharan, J. *When You Can Walk On Water, Take The Boat.* Available: http://www.courses-free.com/spiritual-e-book.html.

Index of /mind-power-articles. Available: http://www.ownyourreality.com/mind-power-articles/.

Lists of True Spiritual Teachers. (2012) Available: http://de.spiritualwiki.org/Hawkins/ListTrueTeachers.

Lundstrom, M. (1996). *A Wink from the Cosmos.* Available: http://www.flowpower.com/synchro.htm. Last accessed 4th Jan 2011.

McNeish, Dr Robert . *LESSONS FROM THE GEESE.* Available: http://suewidemark.com/lessonsgeese.htm. Last accessed 2 Dec 2010.

Meme. (2012). Available: http://en.wiktionary.org/wiki/meme?rdfro. Last accessed 24th July 2011.

My Wage. (2009) Available: http://theinvisiblementor.com/2009/04/01/using-the-poem-my-wage-by-jessie-b-rittenhouse-to-think-differently/. Last accessed 20th Aug 2011.

Paradigm. (2012). Available: http://www.answers.com/topic/paradigm. Last accessed 28th Oct 2011.

Proctor, B. (2011). *Walk Your Talk With Praxis* . Available: www. bobproctordownloads.com. Last accessed 2nd Jan 2012.

Pseudoscience Intelligence Studies. (2012) Available: http://www.answers. com/topic/pseudoscience-intelligence-studies. Last accessed 20th Dec 2011.

Sylvia, C. (2008). *I was given a young man's heart - and started craving beer and Kentucky Fried Chicken. My daughter said I even walked like a man* . Available: http://www.dailymail.co.uk/health/article-558256/ . Last accessed 4th July 2009

The Hundredth Monkey Phenomenon. (2009). Available: http://www. storiesofwisdom.com/the-hundredth-monkey-phenomenon/. Last accessed 4th May 2011.

Widemark, S. (2009). *Lessons From The Geese.* Available: http:// suewidemark.com/lessonsgeese.htm. Last accessed 20th Dec 2011.

Zamora, A. (2012). *The Mind.* Available: http://www.scientificpsychic. com/workbook/chapter5.htm. Last accessed 4th March 2010.

www.ingramcontent.com/pod-product-compliance
Lightning Source LLC
Chambersburg PA
CBHW060305100426
42742CB00011B/1870